HAINT BLUES

HAINT BLUES

Strange tales from the American South

TOBY SELLS

State & Beale

Table of Contents

Chapter 1: Gray Man of Pawley's Island
Chapter 2: Lady Wonder
Chapter 3: Ghost Gumbo Part 1
Chapter 4: Devil Music
Chapter 5: The President and the Witch
Chapter 6: Pascagoula UFO Abduction
Chapter 7: Mysteries of NASCAR
Chapter 8: Past Lives at UVa
Chapter 9: The President and the Honeymooner
Chapter 10: The Lizard Man
Chapter 11: Ghost Gumbo Part 2
Chapter 12: Old-Timey Bigfoot
Chapter 13: Little Green Men of Kentucky
Chapter 14: New Orleans, Of Course
Chapter 15: Haint Blue
Chapter 16: Crypto Gumbo
Chapter 17: Smoky Mountain Ghost Stories
Chapter 18: Haunted Mississippi Gulf Coast
Chapter 19: Flatwoods Monster
Chapter 20: The Witch of Pungo

Dedication

For my wife and our boys.

Copyright © 2024 by Toby Sells

All rights reserved. No part of this book may be reproduced in any manner whatsoever without written permission except in the case of brief quotations embodied in critical articles and reviews.

First Printing, 2024

1

Gray Man of Pawley's Island

A brewing storm

It wasn't raining. Not yet. But the sea air smelled electric, alive. The wind was rising, just like the weatherman said it would. But just then it blew gently, like the cheerful breeze from a box fan.

The man looked out over the sea and sky, now painted together in a dull, limitless void. He knew somewhere out there just miles from where he stood, a deadly storm spun like a top. It had bands of wind that cut like chainsaws and rain enough to bury cities. It was the size of South Carolina. And it was flying straight at him at nearly 100 miles an hour.

It had been all over the radio. Government folks telling him and everyone else on the island to leave. It was mandatory. And he was going to go. But he stalled. He looked one more time from the ocean back to his house.

He wondered if it would be the last time he'd ever see that view from that porch. Maybe he frowned a little and looked down for a moment, resigning himself to some bitter reality he'd better start getting used to. But he looked once more to the sea.

This time he spotted something out among the dunes. Was it gray? He wasn't sure. But there it was, from out of nowhere and completely out of place on the threatened shore of the empty beach.

But that storm was coming. And maybe a moment was all the man had to spare, all the time he had to look at the thing and make the strange piece fit in the puzzle.

So, he moved on to more tangible matters, shuttering the windows and moving those things he could not replace into the car. As bad as he hated to, he had to leave.

As he drove away, maybe he stole one last glance at his beloved home in his rear view mirror. Maybe his thoughts returned, again, to that gray figure on the beach.

But there were potent and powerful worries aplenty. So, maybe the image of the gray figure was pushed back behind thoughts of his insurance policy, or whether or not he'd be able to find a gas station or a place to stay as he evacuated.

But that gray figure would later rise like a beacon in the man's mind. What it foretold was miraculous and as far as the man was concerned, a miracle had indeed occurred.

When the man returned home, he became part of a legend. One that had been told since there were only 24 stars on the American flag. And fresh tales of this legend arrived as late as 2018.

The Gray Man

When a hurricane threatens South Carolina, residents of Pawley's Island keep watch for one man. No, they're not waiting on a politician or a trusted weatherman.

The man they're looking for is barely a man at all. To some he's looked like a man. To one woman, he looked like her lost lover. To others, the man is only a shadow, a shade, a vague form on the dunes that leaves them wondering, *Did I see what I just saw?* And sometimes, only later, they'll have to tell themselves, *Yes, that's what I saw and it's who I thought it was.*

Because when those on Pawley's Island see this man, they know bad news is on the way. They know a hurricane is coming. But, if you've seen the Gray Man, your home will likely be spared from devastation. That's how the story goes anyway.

Why? No one knows. But the tale is locked in Lowcountry lore. Some have tried to explain that it's that romantic silver lining to tragedy that Southerners are always looking for. But events surrounding stories of the Gray Man have been a reality on Pawley's Island for generations.

"Everyone who goes to Pawley's Island and stays for any length of time is bound, sooner or later, to hear something about the 'Gray Man.' If heard from an old timer, the story may be anything from a mere name to a mysterious tale or experience."

That is the beginning of *The Return of the Gray Man*, a book written by Julian Stevenson Bolick and published in 1961. The book captures some of Lowcountry's greatest Gray Man stories, and it does so with amazing sources. But if you plan to pick it up, know that it drips with ugly and just oh-so-casual racism.

Some of the stories in the book are the earliest ever recorded about the Gray Man. They go back to at least 1822, during the John Quincy Adams administration. But Gray Man stories have continued well past Bolick's book, right up to and through the digital age.

For example, in August 2018, a story in the *Myrtle Beach Sun News* recalled the Gray Man legend and called him a "watchful, dead friend" to Pawley's Island. This was months before Hurricane Florence began churning in the South Atlantic. It goes to show how strong the legend remains there. And, as the storm approached, dozens of Gray Man stories and sightings popped up on Twitter and Facebook.

Pawley's Island

Pawley's Island is about 3 miles long and about a quarter of a mile wide. It's a barrier island, separated from the mainland by the Waccamaw River and the Atlantic Ocean. The town sits on South Carolina's coast about 70 miles north of Charleston and 25 miles south of Myrtle Beach. It's on the south end of a string of beach resorts called the Grand Strand.

Drive along sandy Myrtle Avenue and you'll find historic beach homes and a marsh that seems to stretch on forever. Visitors call the town beautiful, the pace slow, the beaches uncrowded, and the overall mood, they say, is tranquil.

Last time the government sent folks to check, they found 107 souls that called Pawley's Island their home. It's mainly residential with some restaurants, shops, and a few hotels. Leisure is the town's major industry. And, if it has one, I'd say history is its major export.

And one bit of the island's history has risen above the rest and carried on through the ages. The funny part is no one can agree on the exact story. It's a ghost story, after all.

Young love

Saltwater sprayed the young man's face as he spurred his horse across the island's soggy sand at low tide. He looked over his shoulder to see his enslaved servant riding up behind him.

The young man had arrived at Pawley's Island only a few hours before. He dutifully paid respects to his family, and then he lit out.

The man was about his business. He'd been abroad for two years and, back on Pawley's Island, he'd left the woman he loved. Having been away so long and now being so close, the man wanted to see his lover as quickly as he could. He had to ask a question. *The* question.

With all of those forces at work, it's understandable that the young man got risky. Well, maybe even a little foolhardy.

Here's how Bolick told it in his book:

"The master took a short cut through a marshy area without giving it much thought. To his horror, the horse lunged forward and he was thrown! Terrified and frantic, he realized they were in quick sand.

"He was sinking and powerless! The poor animal's eyes rolled wildly as it screamed and fought to free itself, but with each movement it sank deeper into the mire.

"The man shouted for his servant, who was there in an instant, untying his bridle as he came. He tried several times to throw the reins to his master but it was too short!

"Realizing this, he ran into the woods in hopes of finding a pole or a sapling that would be long enough. He could find nothing!"

Waiting for the young man to arrive, his lover had the house made up for a royal visit. Flowers were brought in from the gardens, filling the house with the sweet smells of gardenias and camellias. She'd had his favorite meals prepared, all of his favorite meals, as the story goes. I imagine her standing on the second-story balcony, hands on the rails in her most beautiful gown, staring hopefully down the sandy dirt road through a tunnel of live oaks just waiting for her man to arrive.

But, as the story goes, she was left waiting. The servant rode as fast as he could to the young woman's house. But before help could get back to the young man, he died.

For days after, the young woman was stricken with grief and took to walking alone on the beach. The sea mist mingled with her tears as waves crashed on the shore and gulls cawed impolitely at one another.

The gray mist rose off the surf and, through the haze, she could just make out the figure of a man. Was he gray, she wondered, and focused her eyes.

The return

Instinctively, she began moving toward the figure. Now she was sure he was a man, dressed in all gray. Moving even closer, she allowed herself to dream the man resembled someone she knew. Squinting hard into the mist, she swore the man was her lost lover. At ten feet, she was sure. Her lover had miraculously returned and he was standing right there in front of her on Pawley's Island.

Her lover — or, whoever the figure was — never spoke, never moved toward her. She reached out to embrace him but held nothing but sea air and mist. The man in gray disappeared.

That night the woman dreamed. It was a dream she'd had before, in fact. In it, her lost lover had returned to her.

"He was standing on a high dune, calling for her to come to him. But she couldn't. She was in a boat with no oars or a paddle." A storm roiled off in the distance and she slipped farther and farther into its black heart. He called to her but she could not respond, not with all her strength. Instead, her boat carried her farther into the dark waters.

According to Bolick, this was the story she told her father that next morning. The night before, she'd told of him of seeing the man in gray on the beach and that she thought it was her lost love. The father tried to calm her but couldn't. That very next day, the father moved his family from the "island house" back to the plantation house farther inland.

The day after that, a hurricane lashed Pawley's Island. This was 1822 — they didn't name hurricanes back then, but that didn't make them any less brutal. The storm leveled Pawley's Island. Bolick wrote that "people saw lights still burning in houses as they were swept to sea. The loud helpless cries of the inhabitants rang above the furious howling of the winds."

Thanks to the young woman's troubling vision on the beach that day and her troubling dream that night, the family moved inland — and were saved from that terrible storm of 1822. The woman believed that her lover, in the form of the gray man she saw on the beach, came back from the grave to warn her of the gathering storm.

The gray protector

Since that big, unnamed storm, Pawley's Island has been battered by five hurricanes. The man in gray, the Gray Man, has been seen before most of them.

In 1954, Hurricane Hazel had flattened Haiti and locked the South Carolina coast in its sights. Hazel ripped through Pawley's Island. Houses were pulled from their pilings and pushed like toy blocks down the beach. Sailboats were washed together and laid in piles like so many socks waiting to be matched and folded. Homes and lives were scattered up and down the coast. After the sea retreated, Pawley's Island was awash in despair and worry.

From start to finish, Hazel killed nearly 500 people from Haiti to Toronto. The storm was so deadly, the weather service retired the name Hazel for hurricanes.

That brings us back to the man who thought he saw something gray on the beach right before he evacuated. When he returned to the island after Hazel, he found his home intact. More than intact, actually. Everything was just as he'd left it. In fact, the beach towels hanging from the handrails outside had not been moved by winds strong enough to level the rest of the town.

What had only been a tingle in the man's mind became a fact to him in that moment. He had seen the Gray Man, and the mysterious figure had spared the man's family and home.

Flash forward to 1989, Hurricane Hugo had blasted the Caribbean and was tearing an angry streak straight to Pawley's Island. Thousands fled only to come home and find that Hugo had laid chaos upon the peaceful island. Where was the Gray Man, they wondered?

When Jim and Clara Moore returned, they probably found the streets clogged with beach chairs, refrigerators, framed family photos, insulation, and more. But the biggest surprise waited for them at their house.

"I didn't think much about it until the article came out in the paper," Clara told *Unsolved Mysteries* in 1989. She was referring to a story headlined, "The Gray Man fails to appear." "Then we talked about, well, we had seen him."

Two days before Hugo hit, Bob and Clara were taking their afternoon stroll along the beach. No one was out, except one man.

"He was coming directly towards us," Bob said on *Unsolved Mysteries*. "When I got within speaking distance, I thought, well, you always speak to people whether you know them or not. So, I raised my hand to say hi or beautiful evening or beautiful night or whatever."

But the man said nothing in return, a gesture clearly outside the Southern manners of Pawley's Islanders. But what he did next, Bob called it "eerie."

"Of course, I didn't worry too much about it. I said, you know, I was just seeing things. But I'm sure that he was there and when I started to speak, he wasn't there."

Clara said, "I didn't know it was the Gray Man. I just thought it was someone on the beach until he disappeared. I can't explain our good fortune other than the presence of the Gray Man, and the Lord, of course."

Their good fortune? Everything at their house was just as they'd left it before the storm.

Nearly thirty years later, Hurricane Florence was growing in strength over the Atlantic and aimed its 350-mile span at the coast of North Carolina and South Carolina. The storm was so big that astronauts on the International Space Station had to use an extra wide angle lens just to get it all in one frame.

As Florence churned, so, too, did news reporters, trying to get the latest information on the evacuation orders, preparations, and more. And as they dug, some found the Gray Man story.

The legend was retold in the digital pages of the *Atlanta Journal Constitution*, *Mother Jones*, Yahoo News, and on national and local television reports. A few locals claimed on social media to have seen the Gray Man.

By the time Florence made landfall at Wrightsville Beach, North

Carolina, its winds were at 90 miles per hour. About 100 miles south, Pawley's Island officials had prepared for the worst and all but three of the island residents had evacuated. When it was all over, the island was left largely untouched.

Was it the Gray Man? Had he really been seen? Yes, well, maybe.

About a month before the storm, a family vacationed in nearby Horry County. One night they watched a ghostly gray figured walk down a pier toward their hotel.

They watched in amazement for awhile and then the man grabbed his phone and took a photo. It shows a man-sized shadow, a gray shadow, with a rough outline of a head and shoulders that cuts eerily against the black night.

The man would not claim the thing to be a ghost, but he would not rule it out either. He said he didn't know what it was. But he knew what he saw.

So, was this the Gray Man? Did he show up more than month early and a few miles from Pawley's Island? He, or something very much like him, had been photographed just before a hurricane.

Theories abound as to the Gray Man's identity. Was he that tragic lover who fell to his doom? Was he another lover lost at sea who returned only to find his beloved marrying his best friend? That story claims all three threw themselves into the Waccamaw River. Is it George Pawley, who once owned the Island? Is it a Civil War captain whose home has survived all the lashings Mother Nature has thrown at it?

That last one you can check out for yourself. The captain's home is now called The Pelican Inn, and you can stay there. Its website says the inn sits behind the highest dunes on the island and it's protected by a grove of live oaks. All of that protected the inn against Hazel and Hugo. Y'know, if that's what you want to believe.

If you want to see the Gray Man, head up Ocean Highway to "Downtown Pawleys Island." There, you'll find the Gray Man

Gallery. Its the oldest art gallery on the island and has Gray Man prints galore.

2

Lady Wonder

The detectives and the choice

Good Lord, they hated to do it.

If word got out about this thing, they didn't even want to think about the ridicule they'd face. Maybe they'd all laughed about it the first time someone brought it up. But that laughter softened as the days wore on. Somewhere in those days, a flip slowly switched and those jokes turned to consideration and then, finally, into confirmation, and action.

You see, a little boy was missing. So, there was a lot on the line and the clock was ticking. The detectives wanted answers, their bosses — and the community — wanted answers, wanted this little boy found and, hopefully, brought back home to his momma and daddy.

The leads those detectives were chasing were drying up. If they were being honest, they were dry — bone dry — like a creek bed in a drought. And they feared if they didn't act fast and explore every single avenue — no matter how crazy it might've sounded — they may never find that little boy.

So, they were willing to do what few police officers were willing to do back then. While you might hear about it every now and then these days, back then it was largely unheard of.

But there they were — staring the disappearance of that little boy right in the face every day. And this option — this choice they were going to make — might, indeed, bring ridicule upon them. But in the end, they decided they didn't care. Bringing that boy home was more important than that.

These detectives looked for help down South. They sent a man there to consult with a known psychic, maybe the most famous psychic working in America at the time. And, yes, that was an edgy move for law enforcement officials back then.

But the man went. And he got some answers. Not the answers the detectives were looking for. Not at first anyway. You just never could tell when you sought help from a psychic.

And consulting a psychic was one thing. But this psychic was a horse.

Amazing animals

Did you ever have a dog that scratched at the back door just before a storm? Isn't that kind of weird? It's like they know it's coming.

Researchers say, though, that animals don't predict the weather, but they can hear better and smell better than humans. That's how they can detect changes in the atmosphere — sense the low pressure and smell the rain — well before we ever can.

The United States Geological Survey says the earliest anecdotal evidence of animals predicting earthquakes goes back to Greece in 373 BC. Back then, rats, weasels, snakes, and centipedes left their homes and headed for safety several days before a destructive earthquake. Again, it's probably just due to the heightened senses in these animals, but scientists aren't exactly sure.

Before giant waves slammed into Sri Lanka and India in 2005, eyewitnesses said elephants screamed and ran for higher ground, flamingoes left their low-lying breeding grounds, and zoo animals refused to leave their shelters. But, again, researchers told *National*

Geographic that it had more to do with those heightened senses than it did some kind of sixth sense.

But in this story I ain't talking about just heightened senses in an animal. This story goes way beyond that. It also goes way beyond well-documented stories of insanely smart animals, like border collies who can read or gorillas who can use sign language.

No, the gifts shown in this story include telepathy and predicting the future. All of it delivered in a barn stall starting at $1 for three questions. But before you write this all off as some podunk, Southern roadside attraction, consider that this horse could guess women's maiden names, predict the outcome of ball games, and even presidential elections — all with great (but not perfect) accuracy.

Let's load up and head out to Richmond, Virginia to step inside the barn with Lady Wonder, the famous, psychic horse.

The beginning

Her trainer called her, simply, Lady.

She was born in February 1924. The little black foal had three white socks and a white stripe down the middle of her face that ran from mane to muzzle. She was the offspring of siblings and the granddaughter of Saturday — a thoroughbred race horse. So, at times she could be high-strung and anxious. But Lady Wonder was so much more, as the world would find out later.

At two months old, Lady was bought by Richmond-area horse trainer, Claudia Fonda.

"I bought her when she was a very young filly and raised her on a bottle and oatmeal gruel," Fonda told *The Richmond Times Dispatch* in 1952. "The owner said she wasn't going to live and that I was foolish to spend my money that way."

Almost anytime I reference "the newspaper" or paper in this story, I'll be talking about *The Richmond Times Dispatch*. Over the decades — from at least 1938 to 2003 — the paper carried dozens of stories, and columns, and opinion pieces about Lady Wonder.

But as Fonda began to raise Lady, she began to notice something, well, different about her. The first thing she noticed was that Lady would come running to the barn before she'd ever called her. To check the phenomena, Claudia said she began to greatly vary her routine, show up at the barn at vastly different times for feeding, brushing, and the like.

"All they had to do was wish the horse to come," read a story in the newspaper, "and Lady would gallop to the house in short order."

Later, during training sessions, Claudia began to only think of the commands she wanted Lady to follow, instead of calling them out loud. Miraculously, the horse followed them with stunning accuracy, she said.

Claudia recognized the horse's talent. So, she separated her from the other horses. In Lady's patch of the field, Claudia set up a table on which she placed 26 toy blocks, each marked with a different letter of the alphabet. Within months, the horse could easily recognize each letter on the table. She mastered numbers, too.

The early days

They toy blocks worked, I guess, because Claudia and Lady Wonder began to talk. It makes me wonder, if you could talk with a horse, what on earth would you talk about? Plenty, I suppose, because Claudia and Lady soon outgrew those blocks. They moved on to a device Lady would use to talk with the world for the rest of her long life.

Claudia's husband had worked at the old Tredagar Iron Works and knew how to work metal. Together, they conceived a sort of typewriter — as long as a piano — for Lady to use to communicate, and the man built it out of scrap metal.

"The horse communicated by using her nose to nudge two rows of keys capped with sponge rubber," according to the newspaper. "When a key was tapped, it released a bracket, and a tin card emblazoned with a letter or digit flipped up."

At first, the Fondas began to share Lady's amazing gifts with family, friends, and neighbors. Lady began to provide answers that she or the Fondas could not logically have known. Her reputation as a psychic quickly spread. By 1928, the public had come to know Lady as Lady Wonder.

As the public came to press Lady on questions of love, luck, and more, so, too, did the skeptics, out to prove that a psychic horse was impossible and that it was all as ridiculous as it sounded.

In a newspaper story from 1938, columnist Rhea Talley said "soothsaying is a business around Richmond and one that seems to pay pretty well, too." The story described the unusually high license fees "soothsayers" had to pay. They were about $1,000 inside the Richmond city limits versus only $20 Richmond doctors had to pay for license fees each year. Talley also profiled some of the city's noted palmists, phrenologists, and root workers like Madame Lee, Madame Eona, and Master X.

Alongside them all was Lady Wonder, the "mind-reading mare."

"She has a keyboard with all the letters and numbers and by pressing her nose on the keys, she makes the correct letters pop up. The letters are on cards, which slide out and Mrs. Fonda lets anybody switch the cards around before the horse performs.

"Lady Wonder does mind-reading stunts. She will spell out your name. If you think very hard of a certain number, she will press that number. She does all kinds of arithmetic."

In addition to this — and here is the reason Lady was included in this article on soothsayers — "Lady answers questions which concern the future. Ask her, 'Am I going on a trip soon?' And she will spell out 'yes.' Ask, 'When am I going to Norfolk?' She will reply, 'Saturday.'"

According to the story, Master X picked the wrong man in what was then the upcoming boxing match between Joe Louis and Max

Schmelling. Not Lady, though. She went for Louis every time she was asked.

Also, city leaders gave Lady a tax break. Instead of labeling her a "soothsayer" under city code, the Richmond City Council eventually dubbed her "a trained and educated horse," saving the Fondas that $1,000 license fee.

Dr. Rhine's scrutiny

However, Lady's higher public profile brought higher public scrutiny. Just a few years into Lady's life as a public medium, her stall got a visit from Professor Joseph Banks Rhine.

Professor Rhine ran a paranormal research lab in the 1920s at Duke University in North Carolina. It focused on psychic abilities, telepathy, precognition, and psychokinesis. Back then, it was called the Duke University Parapsychology Laboratory. The work hasn't stopped and Duke is still considered a leader in the parapsychology field. It does that work now at the Rhine Research Center on campus in Durham.

Rhine traveled the country in the 1920s investigating and trying to prove or disprove cases of what he called "extrasensory perception," (or ESP), a term he coined.

In 1927, he packed his tent in his car and drove north to Richmond (or what was then a suburb called Chesterfield) and camped right outside the stall of Lady Wonder. Over the next week, Rhine conducted nearly 500 tests of the horse.

According to a story from HuffPost, he started with simple questions: "Can you spell 'boy'?" Or, "What is the cube root of 27?" Then the questions got more complex.

Rhine would write down words in a notebook and he'd hide it from view, both from Lady and from Claudia, who always insisted on being close to Lady during question sessions. Rhine would then ask Lady what word he'd written. He started with simple stuff. But moved onto more complex words like "Carolina" and

"Mesopotamia." Lady guessed them all correctly. In later tests, he would blindfold both Lady and Claudia.

But all of his tests must have proven impressive. After his week at the Fonda farm, Rhine declared that Lady was telepathic. The validation from a well known psychologist was enough to bump Lady Wonder's standing even higher than it had been before.

But it was the horse's amazing feat of 1951 that put her name on newspaper headlines around the country and made her, truly, a national celebrity and a sought-after psychic.

Lady and the missing boy

It had been nearly two years since four-year-old Danny Matson strayed from his home in Quincy, Massachusetts.

In that time, detectives followed every lead and scoured nearly every mile around Quincy. But they turned up nothing. All leads had gone dry. They even offered a $3,000 reward for information on when Danny left home, but neither he nor his body were ever found.

District Attorney Edmund R. Ewing, of Quincy, was tired of it all. He wanted answers, answers for himself, the detectives, his community, but most of all, for Danny Matson's family.

By then, he'd heard the stories. He'd heard of the wonderful things Lady Wonder could do. He'd also heard the exact opposite from skeptical critics. Again, maybe everyone laughed when someone first made mention of this psychic horse in Virginia. But again, Ewing was tired of it all. So, he made the final call.

A friend of his was driving through Richmond and Ewing asked him to make a stop off at the Fonda farm for a little chat with Lady Wonder. He did.

When he got there, the friend asked Lady a simple question. "Where is Danny Matson?" But he got an answer that made him and the law enforcement officials back in Massachusetts scratch their heads a little bit.

Lady told the man to look for Danny in the "Pittsfield Water

Wheel." Ewing said "I thought it meant Pittsfield, Massachusetts," he told the *Times Dispatch* at the time. But he'd already spent $100 in county funds conducting a full but fruitless search of nearby Pittsfield.

He wondered later, though, if Lady meant the "Field and Wilde's Pit," a quarry about 400 yards from Danny's home. It had been searched before, too. But Ewing didn't care. This was the best, newest lead he had. He spent $500, had the quarry drained, and there, lying heartbreakingly at the wet, stone bottom, was the body of Danny Matson.

"It's almost unbelievable but it's true," Ewing told the *United Press* at the time. "We were at our wit's end."

Claudia remembered the man's interview with Lady. She said Lady first told him to look "in water." Then she spelled out "Pittsfield" and the man was very excited, she said.

Lady the national celebrity

The day after the story ran in the *Times Dispatch* about Lady's help finding Danny Matson, the paper said this:

"The world beat a path to Lady Wonder's door yesterday and the mare loved it."

Front pages of newspapers all over the country were splashed with the feats of Richmond's "talking" horse. Television crews flowed in. Newsmen were hurrying south from New York, Chicago, and Canada for a front-row ogle.

It was the biggest day for Lady in her 27 years and she showed it. She worked proudly and swiftly at her big "typewriter," pecking out answers put to her.

Lady was truly on the national stage. And questions from all over the country poured in.

Newspaper reporters asked Lady to identify people missing in their communities. A Texas oilman asked he where he should drill next. A call came from California, asking what horse would win at an upcoming race at San Bruno. A Baltimore woman wanted to know about her mother's will. A Boston woman asked what was Lady's religion.

Lady — or, well, Claudia, I guess — ignored many of these calls. Claudia said the horse would only help those who made the drive to Richmond and appear before Lady in her stall.

But after a day of radio, newspaper, and magazine interviews, Lady was tired. On her typewriter, she wrote a personal message just for Claudia. It read, "go bed."

Missteps along the way

Lady certainly was not right 100 percent of the time. Her picks for the 1952 college football Bowl Games were way off. In fact, only one of the teams she predicted to win was actually playing in either the Rose, Cotton, or Sugar Bowls that year. Asked which team had won the 1951 World Series, Lady answered "Giants." That team hadn't played.

A *Post Dispatch* sports writer wished he'd known about Lady's talents before the football season was over. He said it seemed he was the last in Richmond to know of the psychic horse.

So he did a deep dive on Lady. He chronicled her family tree back to Hanover "one of America's foremost sires," and to a famous mare named "Vacation."

That story said that Claudia had taken Lady to run at the "big race tracks and she'd qualified as a good handicapper." But, the sports writer noted, "Lady's reputation as a crystal-gazer I hear suffered much on account of certain stock market tips."

Also, Lady — like so many other political prognosticators at the time — picked Thomas Dewey to beat Harry Truman in the 1948 presidential election. (He did not.) However, she predicted Dewey would take Virginia. (He did.)

Asked to find another missing boy, Lady gave hope to his parents. She told them the boy was alive and in Kansas of all places.

The boy's body was found about a week later near his home in Rhode Island.

The home stretch

As horses go, Lady Wonder lived a long time. For years, she stood in that barn stall and wowed visitors with the words she typed on that big typewriter.

But in 1957, Lady died of a heart attack in her barn at the age of 33. Her obituary appeared at the top right-hand corner of A2 in the *Times Dispatch* — a place of prominence as newspapers go. In a large font, the paper declared "Heart Attack Fatal to Lady Wonder."

"It was a great shock to us," Claudia said. "She was nice as she could be Saturday night when I put her to bed, gave her a piece of cake and turned off the light. I don't think we'll ever get another horse." Lady was buried the next day in a simple burial ceremony at Pet Memorial Park in Henrico County.

Lady's owner and trainer, Claudia Fonda, passed away two years after her famous horse. Never once did Fonda ever claim that Lady had any psychic abilities. Never once, did Claudia ever admit to any hoax or scam. The paper estimated Fonda hosted some 150,000 people to witness Lady's wonder inside her little barn.

A psychic horse?

Some folks may say, c'mon, Toby, a psychic horse? To those folks, I'll repeat something I've said before — I don't have all the answers. I don't want them. I'm not here to try to debunk anything. Stories in this book live in Southern culture and that's good enough for me.

Nobody alive during Lady's day could prove or disprove any of the horse's abilities. Dr. Rhine, the psychologist from Duke University, later recanted his belief that the horse was psychic. He said he, in fact, believed that Lady's trainer Claudia was somehow signaling the horse to the answers.

But Claudia denied that assertion her whole life, telling the paper that the idea "simply is not so." The day after Danny Matson was found, she said she did not understand herself how Lady was able to answer questions by spelling them out on her typewriter.

"I've often wished I understood," she told the paper. "I'm convinced that there is some strange link between the human and the animal, at least in Lady's case."

If nothing else, Lady Wonder is a fascinating case. And her story is one of a kind and just, oh, so Southern.

3

Ghost Gumbo Part 1

A frightful visit

It was her daughter, flesh and blood. The woman knew it immediately, instinctively in the way parents know their children. But she was further convinced of it because her daughter was wearing the exact same dress she wore the night she was killed.

The mother had been asleep and her daughter appeared to her, right at her bedside. The mother was overjoyed to see her daughter. She remained constantly in her thoughts and prayers in the few days since her daughter was discovered dead on the floor of her kitchen.

The mother was elated to see her daughter, or spirit, or whatever this thing was sitting on her bed again after living so many days without her. But a deep curiosity washed over the mother, too. She propped herself up on one elbow and peered over the side of the bed.

"I wanted to see if there was a coffin, to see if people came in their coffins," her mother told a packed courtroom after the ghostly visit. "But there was not. She was just like she was when she left this world."

The Lord sent her to me, the mother would tell her friends. For she was the only one her daughter could confide in — would confide in— the only one she'd feel comfortable telling her true story.

And the woman told her mother that whole, true story with a simple gesture. When the young woman turned to leave that night, she turned her head completely around on her body.

Southern ghost stories

Ghost stories have been told for so long and told by so many people that they are their own genre — ghost stories. And, in the South, with our reverence of the past and our love of a good story, you can imagine that we've got some pretty dang-good ghost stories.

For two chapters in this book, we're going to feed our souls on a dish I'm calling Southern Ghost Gumbo. In them, I've tried to find some of the best, weirdest ghost stories from all over the South. I'm gonna put them together, and let them simmer. I tried to find some off the beaten path, maybe some stories you've never heard before. We'll touch on some favorites for sure, but we'll also meet a ghost horse in Alabama and a ghost pirate crew cursed to sail the strange waters of the Florida Everglades.

The ghost in the courtroom

For our first story, let's get back to that woman whose joy turned to curiosity and then to fright upon a nighttime visit from her deceased daughter.

The events preceding that frightful night began in November 1896 in the Greenbrier community of West Virginia. That was the year Edward Shue, a blacksmith by trade, married Miss Zona Heaster in the Meadow Bluff area of Greenbrier.

Only a few months later, in January 1897, Edward was on his way to work. Before he got there, he stopped off at the house of a woman he knew and asked her son to go back by his house. Edward wanted the little boy to check the chicken coop for eggs and see if his wife, Zona, needed anything from the store.

The boy followed the directions and diligently checked the coop first but found no eggs. He knocked on the door of the house but got no response. Cautiously, he opened door, and went in.

There, he found Zona's dead body laying across the kitchen floor. She was stretched out perfectly straight with her feet together, one hand lying by her side, and the other lying across her body. And her head was slightly inclined to one side, according to an account from the West Virginia state archives.

The boy had to be terrified. He ran back to his house and told his momma what he'd seen. They both ran to the blacksmith's shop to break the news to Edward. Then they all ran back to the house and got there at about the same time.

They sent for a Dr. J.M. Knapp. By the time the doctor arrived, Zona's body had been laid out, dressed in a dress with a stiff, high collar. And Edward had tied a large veil over her head and under her chin, winding the fabric around several times. According to that account from West Virginia state archives, Dr. Knapp found slight discolorations on the right side of her neck and cheek.

The doctor unfastened Zona's collar and examined the front of the neck and was about to examine the back of the neck when Edward implored him to stop. Dr. Knapp respected the wishes of a grieving husband, packed his things, and he left the house. He ruled that her death was by natural causes. Later, the body was taken to the Meadows and buried.

A few nights later, Zona's grieving mother, Mary, got the first of four frightful, impossible visits from her daughter who — to the rest of the world — lay in the cold ground of the Meadows. She didn't want to tell her mother everything, not at first anyway. But when she finally did, it drove her mother from her grief, into anger, and into action.

After hearing her daughter's harrowing version of the real events of that morning back in January, Mary traveled to Lewisburg and reported it all to prosecuting attorney John Preston. He told her instantly that he did not put much stock in ghost stories. But Mary persisted, and remained so insistent that the prosecutor finally ordered Zona's body to be exhumed.

"It was no dream," Mary said in the trial that followed in July. "She came back and told me Edward was mad. Said that she didn't have no meat cooked for supper.

"The second night she came to me, she told me that her neck was squeezed off at the first joint and it was just as she told me."

And it was. Three doctors, Knapp and Doctors Rupert and McClung, conducted a thorough post-mortem. They found that her neck was "dislocated between the first and second cerebral vertebrae. The ligaments were torn and ruptured. The wind-pipe had been crushed in at a point in the front of the neck."

Edward had been arrested before all of this. And it wasn't all thanks to Zona's ghost. The man had made attempts at resuscitating his wife, though he knew for certain she was dead. But immediately after his Zona's death in his "conversation and conduct," Edward "seemed in good spirits," witnesses said, "and showed no proper appreciation of the loss he sustained." After he received the summons to appear at the inquest in the case and to the post-mortem, Edward told fiends that "he knew he would come under arrest."

On the stand, he denied everything. But he'd bragged to his friends that the state could not ever prove that he did it and believed that circumstantial evidence — such as they had — would not be enough to convict him.

He was wrong. The jury was out for an hour and 10 minutes. When they returned, they convicted Edward "Trout" Shue with murder in the first degree. He was sentenced to life in prison but died after eight years.

While the rest of the world may not remember the names, dates, or places of the now-called Greenbrier Ghost case, the legal world will never forget. This case is the very first in American history in which the testimony of a ghost has been admitted as evidence in a murder-case court room.

Frightful hugs in Alabama

A dark, faceless specter of a woman chases a little boy. A long, dark veil flows out behind her head. Her arms are spread wide to grab at the young boy. His eyes pop. His mouth yawns open in abject terror. His arms fling out before him as he runs for his life.

Head to Alabama and you can see that terrifying image yourself. It's all on a huge sign in plain view with the words "Welcome to Abbeville, Home of Huggin' Molly."

Ghosts, for all we really know and have seen in movies, TV, and YouTube videos, are wispy figures seemingly built from steam or smoke. But not Huggin' Molly. The very essence of this spirit is physical. Heck, it's that physical touch that gives Molly her unique adjective and makes the story one-of-a-kind.

For more than a century, Molly has been reported to be more than seven feet tall, wearing dark clothing, and a broad-brimmed hat. She's big around as a bale of cotton. If you were a child out past curfew, Molly might sneak up behind you, squeeze you tightly, and scream in your ear.

Oh, but that's just something Abbeville parents told their kids, right? They just wanted to get them in after dark and keep them safe, right? No, it surely wasn't to haunt their nightmares for the rest of their lives.

The legend may sound a little strange to anyone outside Abbeville, or nearby Phenix City, or even as far away as Baton Rouge. But Huggin' Molly has a history in all those places.

Over several weeks, newspapers in the early 1800s reported a ghost in Phenix City "of the Huggin' Molly" variety. That meant the ghost was tall, clad in a long, black shroud and long, black veil. She appeared at night and, well, hugged people and screamed in their ears.

Huggin' Molly took root, somehow, in Abbeville and generations of children there have been scared straight by that squeezing specter. But Huggin' Molly ain't always been reported as just fun and games.

The *Guntersville Democrat* (from Alabama) reported in 1912 that Huggin' Molly was a "terror" to some in Pratt City back then.

"It is asserted that 'Molly' will spring upon an unsuspecting victim from some dark corner and hug and squeeze him strenuously," says the story.

One man in police court was charged in Guntersville with carrying a concealed pistol. In his defense, he said he was toting the gun because he was afraid of "Hugging Molly."

If any of this has you wanting to dive deeper into the Huggin' Molly legend, drive into Abbeville for a bite to eat. There, you'll find Huggin' Molly's Restaurant. It's right there on Kirkland Street and has a sort of 1950s-diner vibe.

There, you can get chicken fingers, called Molly's Fingers, served with comeback sauce and fries. Or, get the Screamin' Chicken Supreme with house-made gravy served over white cheddar mashed potatoes.

Story sound far-fetched? Well, Jimmy Rane believes it. He's a lifelong Abbevillian and the businessman behind YellaWood. His dad told Jimmy and his friends that when he was a kid, Huggin' Molly sprung from the shadows one night and hugged him. They were convinced it had to be true.

To this day, hearts beat faster as the moon rises in the sky over Abbeville. Huggin' Molly, dressed all in black, could show up at any time.

A fishing story with a ghost horse

He'd paddled those rivers and creeks for years. He was a guide and had put fish on the lines of colonels, governors, and common folk alike.

But one night he saw something he'd never seen before, barely even knew what he was looking at. From his boat in the middle of the Flint River, it looked like a white horse.

Strange as it was to see a horse — any horse — way out there, it was stranger to see one right on the bank next to his boat at night. He paddled a bit forward, a bit closer. Squinting through the dark, he knew he wasn't seeing it right. He knew how your eyes could play tricks on you.

So, he paddled on a bit, a bit closer to it. The white horse — and that's what it was for sure, he saw then — walked on to keep up with his boat. It was the perfect shape of a horse and as it walked, Dink Melvin could only draw one conclusion: This white horse stepping through the dark of the Flint River at night had no head.

In 1888, newspapers across the South carried this strange tale from Albany, Georgia, in an account headlined "A Fishing Story." It might've been just that, too — a fishing story — but maybe not.

According to *The Wilson Mirror* newspaper in North Carolina, everybody knew Dink Melvin. And if you knew him, you'd probably heard his story of the Headless Horse. He'd seen it for years along the banks of the Flint and the banks of the Muckalee and Kinchafoonee Creeks. Here's the story:

"The ghost that Dink describes most eloquently is in the shape of a big, white horse without a head. The horse is perfect in shape, except it has no head. And Dink says he's been seeing it for the last five or six years.

"Its trysting place is along the river in the vicinity of Fairgrounds and Dink can show it to any man who will go with him after nightfall.

"If he gets in in his boat and rows across the river, the big white horse follows him to a certain place and disappears. It has given him several bad frights, and one Sunday evening as he was returning from the creeks above, the thing came right up to his boat and seemed to be trying to put his fore feet in. Dink says he's been scared a good many times, but this was the worst fright he ever had in his life."

The newspaper reporter heard this story while he was fishing once with old Dink, camped on the bank of the Muckalee.

"I'd just like to see see some man that had the grit to shoot at the thing, but I wouldn't care to be close to him when he done it," Dink said.

To that, the reporter said he'd do it. Others in the camp begged him not to. The man made an appointment with Dink but he begged off, saying he was sick. Dink said he'd call the next day for a another try on the next day. But Dink never showed.

Edisto Island's unsealable tomb

Grief and pain had, once again, brought them back to the church.

Julia Legare had died two years prior; a sudden illness had taken her. She was a wife and mother and she was beautiful, kind, and full of life, so the sting of her death was still sharp.

Her family interred Julia's body in a grand mausoleum beside the Presbyterian Church on Edisto Island, South Carolina. They placed her body inside, said their farewells, and left cemetery caretakers to seal her crypt. But the doors just would not stay shut, no matter how hard they tried.

Two years later, the family returned to the Legare mausoleum. Julia's husband, John, passed away, leaving their son, Hugh, without his momma and daddy. They were going to inter John's body right beside his beloved wife, Julia. But before the ceremony to lay John to rest, those cemetery caretakers made a horrific discovery when they opened the tomb doors.

"Those who buried him said Julia's body was in her crypt, but it stretched toward the mausoleum entrance, her hands curled into claws in front of her to scratch her way out," reads an account of the story from the *Post and Courier* newspaper.

Other versions of the story say dirt in her nostrils showed she was still breathing when she died. But they all agree, Julia Legare had been buried alive.

Here's how the Edisto Beach Historic Preservation Society described it all it in a blog post:

"It is thought that her respiratory and heart rates had dropped so precariously low that they were undetectable by the family"s physician and, so, he declared her dead.

"When she was interred that fateful day, she was merely in a coma, and not dead. This led to the horrible realization that she had woken up in her own tomb, next to the entombed remains of long-dead family members. She was unable to escape and had to wait for her actual death to come and free her of the terror she had woken up to."

After that grim discovery, Julia's family was understandably cautious. They returned to the Presbyterian church just a few days after John's funeral to pay their respects, of course, but to also investigate anything out of place.

When they got there, they must have gasped when they discovered that the mausoleum's door stood wide open. After a brief peek inside, the family members decided the door had just been improperly shut after the funeral. So, they shut it again.

A few weeks later, a clergyman at the church saw that the door was, once again, open wide. He ordered it shut.

"This happened again and again and again throughout the decades," according to the historical society. "Chains and unbreakable locks were used to keep it sealed tight, but they would always break and the door would open."

As little as 50 years ago, a door was put on that could only be removed by industrial, heavy machinery. That door was also opened. It was said at the time that Julia must have been particularly mad at that door because it was not only open but completely unhinged from the mausoleum.

Over the years, thrill-seeking kids and vandals have visited and desecrated the Legare tomb. The family finally moved the bodies to a new location.

Visitors to Edisto Island still find their ways to the Presbyterian Church, specifically to its graveyard, and more specifically, to a doorless tomb. Chiseled above the crypt's entrance in bas relief is the name J.B. Legare.

Ghost pirates sail the Everglades

They died. One by one they perished of fever or starvation. But on they sailed. They had to. Their cruelty won them a curse upon their heads.

So, for the rest of their lives, the crew of pirates were made to forever sail the rivers of water and grass of the Florida Everglades.

This story is old. It's not clear just how old, really. But it was already 300 years old by the time it was picked up by newspapers across the South in 1901. That story is so good, I'd mess it up if I tried to tell you about it. I'm just going to print it right here as I found it. This version was published in 1901 in the Nashville *Tennessean*.

"Down deep in the solitude of the lonely everglades, the sailors say is a ghostly pirate ship doomed to forever cruise about in the muddy bogs and shallow grass-grown lake of the great swamp.

"Three centuries ago, a buccaneering crew that raided the Spanish Main captured a merchant brig off Cape Florida and speedily rifled it of its rich cargo.

"Furious of the length of the chase and the brave resistance of the gallant crew of the merchantmen, the pirate captain cruelly forced every one of the crew to walk the plank. With fiendish ingenuity, the captain, kept the skipper's wife to watch their fate and that of her brave husband.

"She, mad with fear and rage, fell on her knees and, raising her hands above her head, called down the judgement of heaven on the murderers. At that moment, a curling line of foam came sweeping down over the calm expanse and, lifting both vessels in its embrace, carried them both away.

"On, on, the tidal wave bore the pirate ship on its snowy crest. Across the shallows, high over the beach, above the tallest trees. For miles the great wave carried the pirate ship until it finally set it down in the center of the great, pitiless solitude. There, the pirates all soon died of fever and starvation.

"Now, the Indians and hunters in the Everglades tell of seeing the pirate ship with rotting masts and hull and with skeletons manning the threadbare sails — trying to find a channel out of the sawgrass pools into the deep, blue waters of the sea."

4

Devil Music

Down to the crossroads

The man was terrified. He had to be.

It was nearing midnight, but maybe that was hard to tell. Even if he wore a watch, he couldn't see it. Hard to even see your hand in front of your face on a moonless night on a long, straight stretch of nowhere in the Mississippi Delta.

But that dark seemed to grow around him and close in on him as he maybe tried to squint and make out any feature of the endless cotton field that he knew stretched out beside him. But that wasn't any good.

But he knew he was walking. The soles of his worn-out wingtips crunched on that dirt road with every step. The heartbeat cadence of his footsteps would stir a droning beat in his mind and, maybe, he'd zone out for just a minute to the music playing in his head while he walked through that dark. As the music droned on, maybe, his guitar case would arc out on a careless swing, come back and knock him in the knee, and trip him up a little bit.

It was enough to pull him right out of that ethereal droning rhythm and back into the relentless mechanics of thought. There, he could focus on where he was going.

Geographically speaking, he wasn't exactly sure. Spiritually speaking, he was perfectly sure.

To hell, he thought. That's where I'm walking to. After this is done and I'm done, I'm walking straight into hell.

Southern music for the world

If for nothing else, the world can thank the South for music.

Do you like rock-and-roll? Thank the South. What about soul, blues, jazz, country, or bluegrass? Thank the South. While we're at it, don't forget about gospel, folk, cajun, tejano, and zydeco. And, now, we might not have invented hip-hop, but you can thank the South for everything from bounce and trap to crunk and horrorcore.

All of this music has spilled out of the South to every corner of the world. I'm certainly no expert, but it seems all of these Southern styles come from artists willing to try something new, and blend musical traditions.

Think of the way African rhythms met up with German oom-pah sounds in New Orleans. Ever wonder why there's a big, old tuba in funky brass band music? Think of the way Elvis and others blended country music and country blues in Memphis to create rock-and-roll. I may get calls on some of this stuff, but know I'm no expert.

Needless to say, we take music seriously in the South. But how seriously?

Well, some of the folks in this story took their love of music very seriously, upon-their-very-soul seriously.

Whether or not their stories are true, they've left indelible marks in Southern culture. Lemme show you what I mean. Fill in the blanks: In the Mississippi Delta, bluesman Robert Johnson went down to the _____ to _____.

I bet even Southern Sunday school teachers out there easily filled in those blanks, no matter how sinister the answers may be. By now, the story is like Jack and Jill going up the hill, or Little Bo Peep losing her sheep. Robert Johnson went down to crossroads to sell his soul to the devil.

But there's more to that story than you might know and less to that story if you believe historians. And Johnson might not have even been the first bluesman to sell his soul. Well, not Robert anyway, but we'll get to that.

Deals with the devil

Man, the devil's got great stuff, don't he?

Well, it'd seem that way. Because folks have been trading their soul — their most precious and most vital natural resource — to the devil for centuries, even maybe almost 1,300 years.

The Wikipedia entry on "deal with the devil" lays cold steel right at the heart of the matter with a little humor. Here it is:

"The bargain is considered a dangerous one, as the price of the Fiend's service is the wagerer's soul. The tale may have a moralizing end, with eternal damnation for the foolhardy venturer. Conversely, it may have a comic twist, in which a wily peasant outwits the devil, characteristically on a technical point."

That last bit reminds me of those episodes of Andy Griffith where Andy outwits some old city slicker from Mount Pilot or Raleigh.

These deals can also have a third outcome. The person who makes the pact tries to outwit the devil, wins the bet, but ends up in a lifelong tragedy. Like maybe a guy who'd won eternal life but is then sentenced to life in prison.

Yeah, we all may know about Robert Johnson in the early 1900s. But for maybe the first example of someone doing a deal with the devil, let's turn back to the 6th century. That's the 500s, y'all.

A cleric named Theophilus of Adana was unhappy with his position in the church. Instead of turning to God for help, he sold his soul to the devil to improve his station. But he is later redeemed by the Virgin Mary. Theophilus is the predecessor to Faust, maybe the world's best-known soul seller. Though, Faust wouldn't appear for many centuries after Theophilus.

The Faust legend springs from Germany, based on the life of Johann Georg Faust. In the story, Faust is smart and successful but wants more. To get it, he makes a pact with the devil. In exchange for his soul, Faust gets unlimited knowledge and worldly pleasures.

The Faust legend is so widespread, the name has become an adjective. If someone makes a "Faustian" bargain, they're dealing away a part of their honor — their integrity — to get power or success in the short term.

There's a great many in history accused of making such bargains. There was Pope Sylvester II who was said to have made a deal with a female demon named Meridiana to rise to the papacy.

In another deal, according to medieval legend, a monk had broken his monastic vows. He was sentenced to be walled up alive. But, he begged, give him one more night to live and he'd make the most beautiful book to honor the monastery, a book that contained all human knowledge. When morning dawned, there the man sat with a massive tome, beautifully illustrated.

It was impossible, his fellow monks said, to make such a book overnight. Maybe the monk dropped his head a bit at this. "No," he said as the story goes, "I could not do it alone and did not do it alone. I asked for help. I said a prayer, a prayer to Lucifer, the fallen angel, asking him to help me finish the book. The price was mine own soul."

That book, called the Codex Gigas, is still around. It contains a full-page illustration of a demon, a figure squatting over three-toed feet, like lizard feet. Its arms are raised over its head. Fingers spindle out menacingly. Horns, of course, rise over a darkened face with glowing white eyes and a mouth split in a victorious smile. The Codex Gigas is also sometime's called The Devil's Bible.

Fast forward to the 1590s in Scotland, during the North Berwick witch trials. A man named John Fian, a doctor and school teacher, was declared a sorcerer.

As his trial proceeded, Fian confessed to King James that he did, indeed, have a compact with the devil. But he promised he'd renounce that deal and live the rest of his life in service to Christ. That night, Fian said Satan came to him in his jail cell. The devil was wearing all black and holding a white wand.

"Get thee behind me, thou Satan, and start pushing," Fian said he told the devil, "for I have listened too much to thee, and by the same, thou hast undone me, in respect whereof, I will utterly undo you."

To that, the devil said, "That once ere thou die, thou shall be mine."

The devil broke that white wand and vanished.

Fian was given a chance to lead that new life he promised. But I guess he aimed to get a start on that promise sometime later. The same night he was given leniency, Fian stole a key, unlocked his cell, and fled. He was captured and tortured until his execution.

A Bavarian painter, Christoph Haizmann, allegedly signed two pacts with the devil in 1688.

Bernard Fokke, a 17th-century sea captain, sailed so fast that it was said he was in league with the devil. Fokke is also said to be the model for the ghostly captain of the Flying Dutchman.

Jonathan Moulton, a late 1700s militia leader in New Hampshire, was believed to have sold his soul to the devil to have his boots filled with gold coins every month.

Giuseppe Tartini believed his Devil's Trill Sonata, was inspired by the devil's appearance before him in a dream.

Back to the Delta

All right. We've strayed way back in time and far way from the American South.

To bring this story back home, let's get back to that terrified man walking with his guitar case on that dark and lonely road in the Mississippi Delta.

He knew he was bound to burn in the hereafter. For he knew who he sought that night. And it wasn't good. Well, maybe to most folks. But he wasn't most folks. He had a desire, a need. He wanted to play and sing the blues better than anybody in the Delta. It was a burning desire. And he was willing to pay for it. He'd made up his mind on that.

So, there he was. Stepping through the complete darkness of rural Mississippi to meet a man...Wait, was he a man? He wasn't sure. But, then again, it didn't matter. If all went well, he'd do a deal with this...thing.

You might think you know this story. That it was Robert Johnson on his way to meet the devil.

But this story and this man came a generation before Johnson. And chances are, you've met the man at the movies. Well, a fictionalized version of him, anyhow.

The devil and Tommy Johnson

His name was Tommy Johnson. He was born on George Miller's plantation in Terry, Mississippi, in 1896. His uncles and two of his brothers played guitar and other family members played instruments in a brass band.

By the time he was 18, Tommy and his brothers were playing gigs. Later, Johnson moved to Drew, Mississippi, with his first wife, Maggie. There, he met Charley Patton, the Delta's first blues superstar. Johnson, Patton, and others formed a band and they played juke joints in Mississippi, Arkansas, and Louisiana.

Johnson loved the bottle. And it showed in his songs. But it was the bottle — and his addiction to it — that'd ultimately claim his life. That addiction was the subject of Johnson's most-famous song. And, lord, it'll just break you heart.

Johnson recorded "Canned Heat Blues" for the Victor label in

Memphis in 1928. In it, he sings, "Crying canned heat mama, crying sure, Lord, killing me. Takes alcorub (rubbing alcohol) to take these canned heat blues."

The song was about Johnson's habit of occasionally drinking Sterno. Anybody that's worked catering gigs or has been curious enough to look under one of those silver serving dishes on a buffet knows about Sterno. They're usually these little silver cans, about the size of a hockey puck. You pull off the lid and light it and a little flame there will burn for a long time.

What it's burning is a fuel made from denatured and jellied alcohol. Johnson said he'd mix Sterno fuel with water and drink it when other alcoholic beverages were unavailable or too expensive. I said it was heartbreaking, but that practice was common in Prohibition-era homeless camps.

Cub Koda, of "Smokin' in the Boys Room" fame, said, "Next to Son House and Charley Patton, no one was more important to the development of pre-Robert-Johnson, Delta blues than Tommy Johnson.

"Armed with a powerful voice that could go from a growl to an eerie falsetto range and a guitar style that had all of the early figures and licks of the Delta style clearly delineated, Johnson...left behind a body of work that's hard to ignore."

Another Delta musician, Houston Stackhouse, remembered Johnson as an entertainer, "He'd kick the guitar, flip it, turn it back of his head and be playin' it. Then he'd get straddled over it like he was ridin' a mule — pick it that way."

Tommy played music all his life right up to this alcohol-related death in 1956. But what happened to him — what he said happened to him — before he started juking around the Delta made him famous.

His brother, LeDell, taught Tommy the basics of the guitar when he was a young teen. Then Tommy ran away for a few years into the

Delta. When he got back, he'd changed. His guitar came alive under his hands, with a fast fingerpicking style and a bass line to accompany it underneath. He could write songs in a minute. His brother, LeDell, was astounded. How did he do it?

"Now, if Tom was living, he'd tell you," LeDell said in David Evans' 1971 biography of Tommy. "He said the reason he knew so much was because he sold hisself to the devil.

"He said, If you want to learn how to play anything you want to play and learn how to make songs yourself, you take your guitar and you go to where a road crosses that way, where a crossroads is.

"Get there, be sure to get there just a little 'fore 12:00 that night so you'll know you'll be there. You have your guitar and be playing a piece there by yourself [...] A big, black man will walk up there and take your guitar, and he'll tune it. And then he'll play a piece and hand it back to you. That's the way I learned to play anything I want."

If you ever saw *O Brother, Where Art Thou?* — the Coen Brother's 2000 comedy set in Depression-era Mississippi — you met Tommy Johnson, played by Chris Thomas King.

At a crossroads (this time in full daylight), Everett, Pete, and Delmar stop for a man wearing a broad-brimmed hat carrying a guitar case. The man asks, "Are you folks going past Tishimingo?" He gets in, and introduces himself as Tommy Johnson.

"I had to be at that there crossroad at midnight," Tommy tells Delmar in the back seat of the car, "to sell my soul to the devil."

Everett asks him what he got for his soul. Tommy says he taught him how to play the guitar. Delmar scoffs. "Oh, son. For that, you traded your ever-lasting soul?"

Tommy says, "Well, I wasn't using it."

The devil and Robert Johnson

When Tommy Johnson first started playing juke joints with his brothers, Robert Johnson would've been about three years old.

Born in Mississippi, little Robert bopped all over the Delta living at times with his mother and father in Mississippi, Tennessee, and Arkansas. A school friend remembered that at a young age, Robert was great at playing the harmonica and the jaw harp.

When he was 19, Robert married 16-year-old Virginia Travis, who later died in childbirth. Her relatives told musicologist Robert McCormick that her death was Robert's punishment for playing secular music, or "selling his soul to the devil."

But it may be Delta blues musician Son House who is most responsible for seeding Robert's soul-selling story. That story has grown so big over the decades that it almost covers his true talent and impact on American music.

Robert first heard Son House in Robinsonville and wanted to play just like him. According to stories, Robert would always grab House's guitar on set breaks. And he wasn't much good at it.

In a 1997 documentary called *Can't You hear the Wind Howl*, House said, "Folks, they come and say, 'Why don't you go out and make that boy put that thing down? He running us crazy.' Finally he left. He run off from his mother and father, and went over in Arkansas some place or other."

When Robert got back — some say six months later — he'd mastered the guitar. And it raised eyebrows. Some said it was amazing. Others said there was something...supernatural about it.

Blues musicians still remembered the story of Tommy Johnson going down to that crossroads to deal with the devil. And if there was anyone else who had truly laid down their soul — to be able to play like that — it was Robert Johnson.

This was the tale Son House told American music historian Pete Welding one time. Welding went on to repeat the story as a seriously held belief to magazine reporters. And, well, the story kind of stuck.

Truth was — and this is the story that Robert told — he had

studied with a man — a human man — named Ike Zimmerman for all those months. But there was something odd about that, too. Zimmerman, and then Robert, both practiced at night in graveyards, not to conjure demon, but because it was quiet.

However, it got started, it did great things for Robert's career — as it had for Tommy Johnson's. Robert's music took him all over the South and even as far north as New York City and Canada. He was remembered as a guitarist who could play any song after hearing it just once on the radio, according to a story in *Vanity Fair*. His repertoire included songs by Bing Crosby, Irish standards, polkas, and his own blues songs, of course.

And his songs only added fuel to the story about his deal at the crossroads. Consider these lines from "Me and The Devil Blues."

"*Early this morning, when you knocked upon my door.*
And I said, hello, Satan, I believe it's time to go.
Me and the devil was walkin' side by side,
I'm going to beat my woman until I'm satisfied."

The crossroads piece of the story also got a bump from Robert's "Crossroads Blues."

"*I went to the crossroad, fell down on my knees*
Asked the Lord above 'have mercy, now save poor Bob, if you please'"

Historians and critics have said none of Robert Johnson's songs were really about a deal with the devil or about the devil at all. In the music of the time, the devil was just poetic stand-in for sinful ways and sinful people. And the crossroads in "Crossroads Blues" was likely just that metaphoric crossroads we all come to in life, where our lives can take many directions.

Robert died in Greenwood, Mississippi, in August 1938 at 27 years old. Mystery surrounds his death, too, as some claim he was poisoned — murdered — at the Three Forks Store, which was attached to the juke joint he was playing. A sensationalized version of this story claims as he died, Robert got down on all fours and barked like a dog, somehow furthering the claim of his deal with the devil.

It's even a mystery as where Robert is even buried. Go to Greenwood and you can find three headstones for him. One was paid for by Sony Music. Another was erected by the members of ZZ Top. And another is about three miles form the Three Forks Store.

Robert's devil in Mississippi legend and law

No one really knows the real location of the "real" crossroads. But that hasn't stopped Mississippi tourism officials from putting it on the map.

Google it and you'll find a massive monument at the corner of Highways 61 and 49 in Downtown Clarksdale, Mississippi. Three huge, blue guitars angle around a tall pole labeled, simply, The Crossroads. Drive right down 61 and you'll find Crossroads Market and Grill. Drive south on 49 and you'll find Crossroads Furniture. Keep on driving and you'll hit Crossroads Wine and Liquor.

And that crossroads is *the* crossroads, if you believe House Concurrent Resolution 45 passed by the Mississippi House and Senate in 2019. It reads, in part, "Whereas, located at the intersection of Highway 61 ('The Blues Highway') and Highway 49 in Clarksdale, Mississippi, the location where the legendary blues musician Robert Johnson sold his soul to the devil for the ability to play a mean guitar, and formally known as 'The Crossroads,' the land where the blues began..." and that resolution kind of goes on and on like for a time before celebrating the 40th anniversary of the Delta Blues Museum in Clarksdale.

That might be the first time the devil was ever codified in Mississippi law. If it ain't, it's likely the first time the devil was ever mentioned in such a good light down there. But that lawmakers took it that far, shows you just how deep the crossroads and devil legend runs not just in Mississippi or the Delta but anywhere anyone is ever talking about Robert Johnson and the blues.

5

The President and the Witch

The witch letter

He wasn't the president when the letter came.

Things were pretty quiet — quiet for the general anyway — when that letter arrived at his plantation. The rowdiest of his old rough-and-tumble days were behind him. But his biggest fights still lay ahead. He couldn't have known either at the time.

Now, political affairs were simmering. But the pot wasn't boiling yet.

I'm not saying the general was bored (now, nor am I saying he was a really great guy). He was a land speculator, and he was good at it. But a lot of the claims he sold were in territory he'd stolen from Native Americans. As an example of some of his honest land work you may know, the year the letter came, the general and his rich buddies founded the city of Memphis, Tennessee.

Rich, Southern guy back in the day, of course he had a huge cotton plantation to keep him busy. Of course, — lord have mercy y'all and I'm sorry — he bought human beings, stolen from their homelands and he forced them to work his plot against their will.

His biggest battle — the one remembered in history books and songs — was only two years behind him. When the letter came, he'd just returned home from a different series of skirmishes that were

— uh, goodness gracious they were just awful, too. They tainted his name then and now. He still commanded U.S. troops. But he worked, largely, from home. With no major conflicts afoot, the work was regular, routine.

But as he said once, "I was born for the storm, and calm does not suit me." So, maybe he was feeling cooped up. Maybe that's why the letter got him out of the house and on the road. He was comfortable running wars from the saddle. He was happy out with his men and the man never shied from a good fight.

But maybe he acted on the letter because of its plea for help. Its author was the father of three boys who had fought alongside him, and the general was fiercely loyal.

Also, something about the letter rang true. Back then, no man would have sent a letter like that unless he was desperate. The matter had already gotten the man and his family, basically, excommunicated from their church. They'd lost trust from their neighbors and good standing in the community. What could anyone possibly gain from spreading a story like that, especially with a decorated war hero and national politician?

Maybe the supernatural intrigue of the letter just got to the general. He'd heard the stories, sure. Word spread fast, and word like that spread even faster. And, surely, the story had beat the letter to the cotton plantation.

But those were just stories. And there on the general's desk was proof, a handwritten letter from the source and a plea for help. And I bet it was filled with details that curled his hair. And details like that — in that time back then — must have quickened the pulse of any man, even one who had seen so much bloodshed.

I can imagine the general finished the letter's last words, blew out a deep breath, and threw his round reading glasses on his desk. He crossed his legs, leaned back, and ran a hand through that famous mane of wild hair. Maybe he looked out over his fields, and wondered what he should do.

Whatever that letter said and whatever he thought about it, Andrew Jackson became a witch hunter.

The Bells go to Tennessee

In 1810, James Madison was the country's fourth president. That year — and thanks largely to Jackson — parts of West Florida became part of the United States.

That was also the year John Bell moved his large family from North Carolina to Tennessee, which had been a state for 14 years by 1810. There was some speculation about Bell's move further into the frontier — he was running from bad luck, a bad business deal, or bad blood. But, really, it's all speculation.

Bell was an apprentice barrel maker in his youth but turned to farming. He and his wife, Lucy, worked hard and had become some of the most successful planters in Edgecome County in their eight years together in North Carolina.

But — again, for reasons unclear — John decided to pluck his family from that land, move them over the treacherous Appalachian Mountains, and settle them in an area of Tennessee oh-so-attractively called the "Barren Plains."

Robertson County was (and is still) about 50 miles northwest of Jackson's plantation home called the Hermitage, just east of Nashville. The Bell family lived in a Robertson County town now called Adams and grew their farm to a vast 328 acres.

Strange as the circumstances of the move might have been, though, by all accounts, nothing was unusual about the Bells. They were sturdy, independent, and led by their faith.

They also didn't run away from a fight. Three of the Bells' oldest sons, John Bell, Jr., Drewry Bell, and Jesse Bell, were all Tennessee volunteers who served under Jackson at the famous Battle of New Orleans in 1814 and 1815.

But everything their family had built over the years was turned upside one day in 1817 when John saw something strange in his corn field.

Strange beginnings

Now, Southern pioneer folklore is full of ghosts, goblins, haints, hags, lake monsters, and wood boogers. But what John Bell saw that day was unlike much else out there.

Down a corn row, he saw a creature with body of a dog (a German shepherd as the story goes) and the head of a rabbit. And it wasn't afraid of John. The man was able to shoot at the thing four times.

And, remember, this was no automatic rifle. This was a muzzle-loader and them suckers take long time to load. It's about a 10-step process where you load the powder, load the ball, tamp it all down with a ram rod, maybe pour powder under the flintlock, fire, and start all over again. The creature, whatever it was, only disappeared after a fourth shot.

That night, the Bells sat down for dinner and heard something beating and scratching at their door. They were long, slow scratches, not like that of an urgent dog wanting to come inside. Finally, someone got up and flung the door wide open. But they found nothing.

Later, it happened again. So, they devised a plan. If they heard the scratching again, two groups of Bell men would burst out the door and circle the house in opposite directions.

They continued to eat, and I bet it was pretty quiet. Amid the clatter of forks on dinner plates, the scratches returned. The men jumped into action. They rounded the house but all they found outside was each other.

In the days after, they began to hear whispers around the house. And, later, they heard what they described as an old woman singing.

But, then, the spirit got violent. It started in the children's room. They'd hear something like a mouse gnawing on their bedposts.

Later, their blankets would be yanked off them in the middle of the night. Pillows would be ripped from under their heads.

Then the spirit seemed to turn its anger to Betsy Bell, the youngest daughter. The spirit would pull her hair and slap her face so hard it'd leave bruises in the shape of handprints.

The Bells brought in family friend James Johnston for help. He stayed the night and in the morning was convinced something otherworldly lived at the Bell farm. He told John Bell it "was a spirit, just like in the Bible."

It's not clear how word got out. But just like in any small Southern town, word did get out. People began arriving at the Bell farm to experience "the witch" as they called it.

The Bell Witch

Now, "witch" back then didn't really mean a "witch" witch — y'know, green, pointy hat, rides a broom, hates Dorothy, that kind of thing. Though, there was some talk that the spirit could've been some manifestation of a woman, Kate Batts, with whom John had had a bad run in or two. But, really, "witch" just meant something, y'know, bad and unexplainable.

Those folks who showed up at the Bell farm usually got their money's worth. (Well, that's a saying. The Bells didn't sell tickets, and they wouldn't take any money from anybody who'd come as a tourist.) But the longer the spirit hung around, the more amazing its feats became.

It began to speak out loud. It would hold conversations. Later, it repeated — word for word — sermons given on the same Sunday morning but given 13 miles apart. It would imitate people's loved ones, loved one's who'd never laid eyes on the Bell farm.

The spirt also proved to love the Bells. Well, some of them. At one time, the witch helped save the Bell children playing at a nearby creek. She also loved John Bell's wife, Lucy. The witch called her the "most perfect woman to ever walk the earth" and would give her fruit — yes, make fruit appear out of thin air — and sing her hymns.

But the witch hated John Bell, and promised to one day kill "Old Jack," as she called him. It's unclear, really why she hated John, but if I were him and heard this kind of talk from a spirit who'd proven so powerful, I might reach out for help, too.

Maybe that's when he wrote that letter to Andrew Jackson.

Jackson, the witch hunter

Again, whatever was in that letter, made Jackson — only two years after becoming a national hero for his win against the British in the Battle of New Orleans — load up a bunch of rowdies to go hunt the Bell Witch. But loading up a bunch of rowdies and doing anything at all fits so perfectly into what we know of the nature of Jackson.

When he was younger, he and his entourage would head into Nashville and wreak absolute havoc in the riverside taverns, drinking, fighting, gambling, and whatever else you could cook up in the early 1800s.

Jackson — one of the most influential presidents of these United States (and I'm not saying that's necessarily a good thing) — was in three duels that history knows about.

One time, he was crossing the civic square in Knoxville when he passed the governor of Tennessee, Jackson's boss at the time. The governor — John Sevier — had just beaten one of Jackson's buddies in an election. Well, Sevier said something ugly about Jackson's beloved wife, Rachel, and Jackson lost it.

Jackson pulled his pistol and fired on the man. Let that sink in. Andrew Jackson pulled a gun and shot at his boss — the governor of the state of Tennessee — in a very public place in one of the state's biggest cities. He wasn't arrested either. The two dueled later but agreed not to kill each other because they were gentlemen.

Another time, Jackson threw a house party and it got so rowdy he had to escape out of a window. That party was his inauguration party at the White House.

With no war to fight and not much going on at the plantation, maybe Jackson thought hunting a witch out in the woods sounded like a great diversion. In the group he organized was one man who fancied himself a ghost hunter and a witch tamer. (Keep an eye on him for later.)

Jackson and his men all loaded up and headed out. They got to Adams. But before they arrived at the Bell Farm, Jackson's carriage stopped on a wooded path. The horses were fine and the wheels weren't stuck. They just couldn't move.

Jackson got out to assess the situation, and, after a few unsuccessful tries of getting unstuck, he bellowed, "By the eternal, it must be the Bell Witch." Maybe they all laughed, but they didn't laugh long. They heard whispers in the woods and a voice hissed back at them, "You may pass, general, and I'll see you later tonight." With that, the carriage was allowed to carry on.

They got to the Bell house and, for the first few hours, Jackson and his crew were disappointed. They ate dinner and John Bell regaled them with stories about the witch.

Remember the self-described ghost hunter and witch tamer? Well, if you mix good-old boy (for which he surely was), insufferable braggart, total weirdo, and homemade liquor (for which their surely was), you get trouble.

The story goes that this old boy started hollering that his pistol was loaded with silver bullets and that that the Bell Witch was staying away because she was afraid of him. Bad move.

He immediately fell to the floor, twisting, writhing, and convulsing uncontrollably. He was shouting that pins were stuck all over his body. Finally, he was stood up by an unseen force, dragged to the door, and kicked in the pants out into the yard. The witch hissed again, "The tamer is just one of two frauds in this house tonight."

Now, I don't care what kind of rough-neck rowdy bar brawler you are back in Nashville, but after you witness something like that, I wouldn't want to stick around to see if the Bell Witch thought I was the other fraud.

Jackson's men begged him to leave. He wouldn't. No surprise there, at all. But he agreed that all the men should stay awake the rest of the night to see if the witch ever came back. She didn't. And in the morning Jackson and his men, with their curiosity apparently satisfied, "made all deliberate haste back to Nashville."

The Bell Witch legacy

The Jackson incident hardly covers the breadth and depth of the Bell Witch legend. The unexplained was commonplace around the farm and a nearby cave for decades, and right on up to the present.

Bob Bell, a descendant who now owns a funeral home around Nashville, told Bell Farm tourists in a 2014 YouTube video that the house was sort of a paranormal epicenter.

His grandparents were still living on the property when he was a kid. And, once, his grandmother found her bone China perfectly arranged on the living room floor. The China had been locked away in a heavy trunk. His grandfather once saw the specter of a horse-drawn carriage around the nearby cemetery. The carriage had no driver.

The farm, house, and cave have been featured on just about all of the spooky television shows you can think of. The story has been told in several films. It's considered by many to be the most well-known (and maybe most-told) ghost story in America.

Fueled by the legend, the Bell Farm is now a full-blown, bless-our-hearts tourist attraction. Around Halloween, you can celebrate Bell Witch Fest at the home and grounds in Adams. The gift shop there offers books, hats, and refrigerator magnets. A cave and cabin combo tour ticket will set you back $18. In the summer months, the

Bell Witch Cave Canoe Co. will rent you a tube or a boat for a day-long float down the Red River, which runs right by the Bell farm.

Is the Andrew Jackson story true? Who knows? I don't. The story first appeared in print in an 1894 letter from an attorney who said he'd heard it from his great grandfather. Though, the Jackson and Bell Witch tale is one that historians at the Hermitage love to tell around Halloween.

6

Pascagoula UFO Abduction

A fishing story

In 1973, these two old boys from Mississippi went fishing.

It might not sound like much, but the events of that night divided these boys' lives in two pieces. Things happened before. Things happened after. The tiny threads that bind those two pieces together, maybe as little as 20 minutes, made international headlines and forever changed those two old boys and their part of the Gulf Coast.

After Charlie Hickson and Calvin Parker went fishing that October Thursday in Pascagoula, Mississippi, they came home different, and they'd be different from then on. Theirs was a tale hardly anyone could believe, one that many did not believe. But one — whether you believe it or not — that remains a mystery to this day.

Yeah, it changed those boys, but it changed them in different ways. And you could tell that from the beginning. It's plain to anybody who ever saw this famous newspaper photo of the two men at the time.

They're sitting together on a couch in the Jackson County Sheriff's Office. Young Calvin's arms are crossed. His head is down. His eyes stare off, unfocused into the distance. You can tell he's a million miles away, wishing he could be a million miles away.

But Charlie's bald head is up. His clear, piercing eyes are giving a look that says, I know this sounds crazy but you have got to believe me. By god, you'd better believe me.

Deputies got Calvin and Charlie's full story that night. Then they left them alone in the interview room together. See, the cops had a secret and they were gonna bust these boys, these hoaxers. But it backfired.

In that room alone, Charlie told Calvin, "I thought I'd been through enough hell on this earth and then to go through something like this. Something like this, you can't get over it in a lifetime."

Calvin and Charlie before

Charlie was older. Back in '73, he was 42 and Calvin was 18. But they both worked together there at the F. B. Walker Shipyard in Pascagoula. Called Mississippi's Flagship City, Pascagoula sits right on the Gulf of Mexico in between Biloxi and Mobile, Alabama. There at the shipyard, Charlie and Calvin's company built tugs, towboats, and fishing boats.

Charlie was a foreman and it's been said that Calvin looked up to him, kind of like a dad. While they both worked in Pascagoula, they were both from up north around Hattiesburg.

They got to talking at work that Thursday and decided that they'd go fishing right after they got off. When the whistle blew, they loaded their gear into Calvin's brand new AMC Hornet. They drove to a spot on the Pascagoula River down by an old grain elevator.

At first, they were after hardheads and croakers, and they caught a few. But Charlie convinced Calvin to move. He said he'd caught redfish and speckled trout out by the old Shaupeter Shipyard, right off Highway 90. After a brief drive, they were back at the river bank. They unloaded their gear and made for an old iron pier right over the water.

The October air was cool and clean with that Gulf breeze blowing on them. Probably all you could hear were the sounds of the boys' spinning rods and maybe a low hum coming from the shipyards nearby. I bet it was so peaceful...until they saw it.

"Them"

They spotted a blue light, maybe two or three miles away, and it surprised them. Lights in the sky weren't unusual, but a blue light? It caught their attention.

Charlie said, "Then it in just a little while, it come right down above the bayou."

The blue light got closer, 25 yards or so and those two boys got scared. Then they were able to see it was an oval-shaped craft that had that strange blue light on the front of it. It went over their heads and came to hover right behind them close to Calvin's car. They said it was oblong and about eight feet tall. Calvin said he "liked to've had a heart attack." And I don't blame him.

They described the sound it made the same way for decades. It was a buzzing sound or a zipping sound or a long hiss. *Nnnnnnnn. Nnnnnnn.* Or, *Zzzzzz, zzzzz. Ssss. Ssss.* And there was no big blast coming from it like from a rocket would have, Charlie said.

They just stood there, watching it. Then one end of the craft opened up and three of "them" just floated out. They were about five feet tall. With pale, gray skin, like elephant skin, the brothers said. A cone shape came out of their faces where a human nose would've been. Below that was a slit like a mouth, but it never moved. They seemed robotic.

Charlie didn't see any eyes. But they had something on each side of their heads that kind of looked like ears. They didn't have necks; their heads just rested on their bodies.

Charlie told police the figures glided — not walked but glided — out of the ship and moved right up toward them and there was nothing they could do about it. Charlie said, "I was scared to death. And me with a spinnin' reel out there — it's all I had."

The figures glided up and around Charlie and Calvin. Both

had been paralyzed, either by fear or by some unseen force. They grabbed the men under the arms with hands that looked like pinchers. Calvin said his arms froze up, "just like I stepped on a rattlesnake." With no force at all, they lifted the men off the ground.

"And they glided me into that thing," Charlie told police. "You know, how you just guide somebody? All of us moved like we were floatin' through air.

"When I got in there, they had me, you know, they just kind of had me there. There were no seats, no chain, they just moved me around.

"I couldn't resist them. I just floated. Felt no sensation, no pain. They kept me in one position a little while, then they'd raise me back up."

Both boys said the inside of the craft glowed brightly, but neither could find a source of the light.

Then an instrument neither man had ever seen before was set before them. The only way Charlie could describe it was that it looked like a big eye. It began to scan their bodies, up and down.

Then the beings would leave for a time. They'd return and continue to scan. Then leave. Charlie said he wasn't even sure if he was conscious, though he thought he was. If he was, he could only move his eyes, he said.

He even tried talking to them. "I'd get a buzzing sound out of one of 'em. That's all. They didn't pay me no attention, my talking or nothing."

Charlie said Calvin kind of passed out when the beings first grabbed them. But Charlie might've just been covering for him. You see, Calvin didn't want to talk. He was afraid if they did talk, "they'll come back for us."

When they were released by the beings, the two only remember standing on the bank of the river where they'd been before. There was no handshake. No hug. No butter bowl filled with leftovers. Just, poof.

Well, not just poof, I guess. There was that buzzing sound again and the craft was gone. But not before it shattered every window in Calvin's brand-new car.

And, then, Calvin and Charlie were alone again, right back on the bank of the Pascagoula River, nice and peaceful.

The two weren't sure how long they'd been in there. Could've been three hours or could've been 20 minutes, Charlie said. He didn't know because he never wore a watch. But he was sure about one thing.

He said, "I've never seen that sort of fear on a man's face as I saw on Calvin's. It took me awhile to get him back to his senses, and the first thing I told him was, son, ain't nobody gonna believe this."

Neither man had been drinking before the incident. Calvin didn't drink at all. But once they were back on the ground, Charlie leaned against Calvin's car and nipped on a bottle of whiskey. And I don't blame him.

The tale on tape

At first they weren't going to tell anybody. But once Charlie collected himself, he decided that somebody, somebody official, ought to hear their story. Charlie was afraid that what had happened to them might be the first volley in a full-scale alien invasion.

They called Keesler Air Force Base but were told to call the local police. Fearing that the police wouldn't believe them, the two drove over to the office of the *The Mississippi Press*, the daily newspaper there in Pascagoula.

It was late and the reporters were all gone. But Katherine and Dorothy Smith were inside the office cleaning up. Charlie came up banging on the door. They told him he couldn't come in and that he needed to go to the police. But Charlie must have told them what happened, because Dorothy and Katherine said they were skeptical.

"He didn't seem like he'd seen nothing," Katherine told a TV news station at the time. "He seemed calm. He didn't seem frightened."

Dorothy put it plainer. "I think they'd had a drink," she said.

The two men finally decided to take their story to the police. Well, maybe Charlie decided that. A detective working that night said Calvin came in crying, begging Charlie not to talk, again, for fear "they" would come back for them.

But the two finally did talk with Sheriff Fred Diamond. Charlie told the sheriff he was afraid the police wouldn't believe them. Diamond asked, "Well, how'd you know unless you tried?" Charlie apologized.

Charlie said he didn't want publicity. Both of them said they didn't want to upset their families. Diamond agreed and asked them to come back the next day and make a full statement.

Then the police left Calvin and Charlie in the interview room alone. But they didn't tell them they'd left a hidden tape recorder running.

Diamond and detectives hoped the two would get to talking. Hoped they'd say, "We got 'em. They're believing this crazy fishing story hook, line, and sinker!"

But they didn't. In fact, their conversation on that tape became one of the most convincing pieces of evidence for their story.

Here's how some of that conversation went:

CALVIN: "I got to get home and get to bed or get some nerve pills or see the doctor or something. I can't stand it. I'm about to go half crazy.

"You see how that door just come right up?"

CHARLIE: "I don't know how it opened, son. I don't know."

"They won't believe it. They're gonna believe it one of these days. Might be too late.

"I knew all along they was people from other worlds up there. I knew it all along. But I never thought it would happen to me."

After a pause, Charlie said he was going to have to get a drink when he got home to help him sleep. Calvin said he wanted to go home and that he was getting sick.

With that, Charlie got up and left the room. In there all by himself, Calvin began to pray.

"It's hard to believe," he said. "Oh, God, it's awful...I know there's a God up there..."

Then the tape ended.

The story blazes in public

Glenn Ryder, a deputy, laughed at the two boys that night. Nearly four decades later, he told a newspaper reporter, "I don't know what happened to them. I wasn't there with them, but I know you don't fake fear, and they were fearful. They were fearful."

Later, Calvin and Charlie underwent a thorough battery of examinations, by humans this time. They were psychoanalyzed, hypnotized, given physicals, and both passed a lie detector test. No one could prove they were lying.

Newspapers grabbed the story with both hands. Within days, reporters from all over the world converged on Pascagoula. They all told the same story: Two local fisherman were abducted by aliens.

A Mobile television station said a psychic had predicted a UFO appearance and they were going to show it live. About 1,000 cars showed up at the site but nothing happened.

Nearby in Ocean Springs, an alderman wanted a rule against operating a UFO at more than twice the speed of light on Highway 90. Another wanted to make it illegal to land a UFO in the city limits. The mayor voted against it all, saying he didn't want to discourage tourism.

Some in Pascagoula thought it was all bull. Maybe others had their eyes on the skies. A TV news reporter said he'd heard others say — and oh my god this is so beautifully Mississippi — "We're having a party at the house tonight with shotguns on the front porch. And if them suckers land here, we're going to shoot 'em."

Calvin and Charlie after

While everyone else was having fun, Charlie and Calvin were taking the first turns into what would be the rest of their lives.

Charlie told anyone who would listen. In the process, he became a bit of a Gulf Coast celebrity. He did TV interviews, got letters from all over the world, and appeared in a UFO documentary.

In 1983 he wrote and self-published a book called *UFO Contact at Pascagoula*. Charlie appeared at UFO conventions and even directed a film about his abduction called *In Contact*.

Ah, but, Calvin, he ran. He chased oil jobs and construction jobs. If somebody at work figured out who he was, he said he'd just move on find another job, another town.

But he was always found out and that could only last so long. So, later, he tried to lean into the story, too, maybe trying to own what happened to him. He made several television spots about UFOs and his own abduction. But later, he just gave it all up and headed back to the Gulf Coast.

In a 2013 interview with *The Associated Press*, Calvin said he was still recognized. Also, noting that he's a man of God, Calvin wondered if the creatures that grabbed him that night weren't aliens at all, but demons.

In 2018, Calvin told the *Clarion-Ledger*, the daily paper there in Jackson, that he'd finally changed his mind about keeping quiet. He'd attended a funeral, was immediately recognized, and left out respect for the family, saying people were making the funeral more about him than about the deceased. He'd spent 45 years not talking about the thing that defined his life and the time had come.

"I felt like everyone deserved an explanation," Parker said in the interview. "Everyone has an expiration date, and I wanted to get this out there before I die."

So, he did. Parker lays everything about his abduction and his life after in his book "Pascagoula, The Closest Encounter — My Story."

"I catch myself going fishing at night and look up and wonder where they came from and how far did they travel and why they had to get me," he said.

In that 2013 story in The Associated Press, Charlie's son, Eddie, said his dad spent the rest of his life trying to let everyone know that we're not alone. Charlie died in 2011 at the age of 80.

New witnesses come forward

Good thing it was a nice, clear night. It was October and that hot humid, Mississippi summer weather was finally on its way out. It seemed to blow right over Pascagoula and off into the Gulf somewhere.

And that was a good thing because all she could do was sit there and wait. She'd driven her husband down to the dock. There, he'd meet the captain and the boat that would take him offshore to work. But at the moment, her husband was snoring softly in the passenger's seat.

It was 1973 and the woman didn't have a smartphone to look at. And with her husband sleeping, she probably didn't want to turn on the radio. So, the woman just sat and looked down over at the Pascagoula River, maybe listening to the water and the low, industrial hum coming from the nearby shipyards. Then she looked up at the black sky, scanning through all of those beautiful stars until she found the Big Dipper.

That's when she saw it. A blue light was rising over the river. Now, lights in the sky weren't unusual. But a blue light? It caught her attention. At first, she thought it was a plane or a helicopter.

With little else to do, the woman watched the light. It was moving, slowly, slightly but never made a sound. She woke her husband and they watched together. The craft moved around silently for about 30 minutes, she said. Then it went quickly out of sight.

But the man was leaving and leaving for a long time. So, the couple had other, more terrestrial matters on their minds. They collected the man's clothes from the trunk and walked them down the pier and put them on the boat. Then something else caught their attention.

"We heard this loud, thumping splash in the river," the woman told a newspaper reporter in 2019. "I looked over the side of the pier, and that's when I thought I saw a person in the river.

"I was looking right down on it. It looked like a person [she said maybe in some sort of diving gear], but there was something different about it," she said. "It only came to the surface of the water. As soon as I saw it, it just went back down in the water."

For years, the UFO experience shared by Calvin and Charlie seemed isolated to them. But in 2019, three new witnesses came forth to say they'd seen that same blue light and more on the night Calvin and Charlie were taken.

Maria and Jerry Blair told *The Clarion Ledger* newspaper that on that night they were waiting in their 1969 Pontiac GTO in the parking lot of Graham's Seafood. They were right across the river from were Calvin and Charlie were fishing. That's where the Blair saw that blue light in the night sky.

Jerry got on the boat and went on to work that night. Maria returned home. In the days that followed, Maria heard news reports of Calvin and Charlie's experience. The aliens they described seemed to match what she had seen in the water.

"I thought it was a person," Maria said later. "But now I think it was an alien."

Another woman, Judy Branning, told the newspaper that on that night, four people — her, her roommate, and their dates — were waiting at a red light. That's when the four of them saw something they thought was an airplane. But as it got closer, they knew they were wrong. This thing didn't make any noise and it had bright, bright lights, she said.

"It got closer and it was hovering," she told the paper. "It was kind of a saucer shape or disc shape with a rounded top. The radio started sounding like it was running through all the stations and the car went dead. We were freaking out."

The craft passed right over the car and shot straight up in the air at an incredible speed.

The four agreed not to ever tell anyone else. But Branning said she did tell a few people over the years. But when she talked to the newspaper reporter in 2019, she said she was 74 years old and didn't care if people believe her or not.

"The story is very true," she told *The Clarion Ledger*. "That's what has bothered me for 45 years. It's been on my mind for 45 years."

My heart sung when I read this story. My first thought went out to Calvin. He's lived with this story most of his entire adult life. And, with Charlie gone, he had to feel mighty alone with it. But now, with other witnesses coming along, maybe he can find a little peace about it all.

Also in 2019, officials in Pascagoula put up a historical marker near the site where Calvin and Charlie said they were taken.

The town celebrates

Charlie and Calvin's story is considered one of the most influential UFO sightings in American history. And, in 2016, Pascagoula celebrated it. The town turned out for a Halloween event called Galactic Adventure. It was just before the homecoming football game.

According to Biloxi's *Sun Herald* newspaper, the event featured a costume contest, an electric light parade, the Great Haunted Halloween Bicycle Tour, and a pumpkin pottery demonstration. Folks who had been around back when Calvin and Charlie were abducted were expected to gather at Downton Buffet to share memories.

Scranton's restaurant offered a $4 mixed drink called Absolut Alien Abductions. They had Deep Fried Milky Way Bars for $1. And they also offered something called Paranormal Pork Rinds. Anybody who spent $25 at Ali's Gifts and More got a free Halloween tote bag. Anything space-related at Whimsy's Books & Toys was 15 percent off.

I respect Calvin and Charlie. I never met them but they don't seem like the kind of guys who'd make up something like this. Why on Earth would two blue-collar, Southern boys turn their lives upside down like that? And over something as crazy as an alien abduction? I can tell you, you don't.

7

Mysteries of NASCAR

"**Someone pulled me out that car.**"

His first word was bull...hockey. (Except he didn't say hockey.) But that was the very first thing the man said when they told him at the hospital that no one helped him out of the flaming car.

His crash was caught by a bank of television cameras and it played out in front of a crowd of thousands. The man was an internationally recognized motorsports superstar. His father was nothing short of a racing legend. So, it wasn't like no one was paying attention to the man that Sunday in Sonoma, California. All eyes were on him — certainly if he crashed his car and especially if it caught on fire.

He'd seen the footage. And he admitted he couldn't remember much from the time he unbuckled his harness to the time he was laying on the ground. Still, he was unmoved on that one point.

"Someone pulled me out of that car," he'd say later. He said could even feel someone's hands under his armpits.

After the wreck, the thing was kind of laughed off. The driver said he'd buy dinner for the person who pulled him out. Then, a few months later in a interview on *60 Minutes*, the man said he believed someone was there with him that day and that maybe it was his late father that helped him out of the car.

Fast forward 14 years to 2018, and headlines for stories in *People* magazine and *USA Today* would call the whole thing a "paranormal encounter" and that the man was saved by a ghost. But, then, maybe that's how NASCAR legends are born.

The South's sport is born

If baseball is as American as apple pie, and momma, then NASCAR is as Southern as white liquor and Dirty South hip-hop. If you're trying to remember correctly, you're right. NASCAR really did begin with bootleggers outrunning the law in the Appalachian Mountains.

Prohibition was on and people still liked to, y'know, get drunk. Economists might call that a market opportunity. So, armed with some backwoods know-how, mountain folk made moonshine — mountain dew, hooch, white lightning, and, yes, white liquor.

Product in hand is one thing. Product distribution is another. Without FedEx, moonshiners had to do it themselves. The one thing they knew? Their cars had to be fast and good. During Prohibition their cars had to be better than anything the police were driving, and after they had to better than the IRS revenue men.

Small cars, especially V-8 Ford coupes, were popular among bootleggers. They'd soup up the engines and would sometimes replace them altogether with engines from a truck or an ambulance. They'd build up the cars' suspension systems to handle the turns on country roads and to make the car look normal, not like it was sagging under the weight of 1,000 pounds of illegal moonshine liquor.

And you'd better believe these moonshine runners were proud of their cars. Think of the way Han Solo bragged on the *Millennium Falcon*. The Kessel Run in less than 12 parsecs, remember?

So, after they were done outrunning the law, the only natural next step for moonshine cars was a race, right? And they did. Pastures and backroads became race tracks.

According to the Historic Vehicle Association, a race at the

Atlanta Lakewood Speedway became the first to accept "known" bootleggers right after WWII. Before some races, though, promoters would ban some drivers if they had a history of liquor law offenses. They were afraid these "outlaws" would tarnish the image of their events.

Auto racing had caught on in the South, especially in the Wilkes County area of western North Carolina. And new speed records were being set all the time down in Daytona Beach, Florida. That's where British daredevil Sir Henry Seagrave was the first to reach 200 miles per hours in an automobile. And in 1929 he pushed his famous Golden Arrow to 231 miles per hours at Daytona.

The first official race at Daytona was in March 1936. It ran two miles on the paved A1A, and made a sandy turn onto the hard-packed beach. That's right. For part of the race, he race was right on the beach for two miles until the next turn back onto A1A. (That makes an oval, you see, and in NASCAR...well, you get it.)

For that race, 27 drivers brought a collection of coupes, hardtops, convertibles, and sports cars. Only 10 were left when officials called the race 10 miles short of the scheduled 250-mile distance.

Those cars were stock cars. Stock cars are, really, any car the public can buy off the showroom floor. Stock cars for racing have the same basic chassis as those off the assembly line but with those souped up engines. In NASCAR's early years, some of the cars were so "stock" that it was common for the drivers to drive themselves to the competitions in the car that they were going to run in the race.

After that first race at Daytona, stock car racing got more organized. In 1947, Bill France founded the "National Championship Stock Car Circuit." Later, a mechanic named Red Vogt dubbed it the National Association for Stock Car Auto Racing — NASCAR. And the South's sport was born.

Thousands of races, millions of fans, millions of miles, tankers of high-test gas, zillions of dollars, and dozens of boogity, boogity, boogities later, NASCAR has established itself as a powerhouse in sports, business, and Southern culture.

The Talladega curse

When it comes to NASCAR's tracks, they don't come bigger than Talladega Superspeedway. Established in 1969, the track at Talladega, Alabama, is 2.66 miles long, making it NASCAR's longest and fastest track.

But it's more than racing dynamics that give Talladega mythical standing in the world of NASCAR. Over the decades, the track has been home to scores of mysteries, crimes, fatal tragedies, and the unexplainable. NASCAR fans call it, "The Talladega Curse." Drivers tend to call it the "The Talladega Jinx."

All right, here's two of the favorite origin stories for the Talladega Curse. Some say a local Native American tribe held horse races in the valley where the track now stands. During a race, a chief was thrown from his horse and died. Another story says a shaman put a curse on the valley. That curse came after the local Talladega tribe was driven out by the Creek nation for collaborating with Andrew Jackson.

A *USA Today* story in 2013 was headlined: "Talladega's past filled with death, destruction." That story starts like this: "There is an inherently portentous — some might say sinister — side to Talladega Superspeedway."

The Talladega 500

If you're looking for an example, there's no better place to start than the 1973 running of the Talladega 500.

You know those stickers you see all over NASCAR race cars? Logos for everything from M&M's to Interstate Batteries are plastered all over them. Well, that's not how it was in the beginning. And when Larry Smith did it, other drivers turned up their noses at him. But he didn't care. Carling Black Label beer was paying him to race and keeping his team afloat. Those others drivers would come around soon enough, as we all now know.

Smith was driving his black No. 92 Mercury that day at Talladega in 1973. After just 13 laps, he wrecked. He hit the retaining wall on turn 1. At the time, folks thought it was a minor accident. The car coasted gently to the safety apron around turn 2, and commentators believed at the time that Smith was gliding it there on his own power.

But later estimates found that Smith likely hit the wall at around 180 miles per hour. He was carried away from his car on a stretcher. His black, No. 92 Mercury was towed away and the glass was swept off the track.

Smith's crew chief was certain he could get the car back on the track. But Smith was pronounced dead on arrival at the track's hospital. His death was announced to the fans at Talladega at lap 40. Smith was the track's first fatality.

In a dark twist of fate, Smith and his car graced the cover of *Stock Car Racing* magazine that was on the stands at the time of his death. In the story, Smith talked about being a cautious driver behind the wheel of his personal vehicle. His career was up and running, he said, and he couldn't afford to get hurt in an auto accident.

Later, in that very same race, another event fed fuel to the famed Talladega Curse. The story has taken on a slightly paranormal edge over the years, pushing the curse deeper into racing legend.

Bobby Isaac was an amazing driver. There was no doubt about that. He set 28 land speed records at the Bonneville Speed Flats in Utah. But it's also been said that Isaac was an impulsive man.

Nothing seemed out of the ordinary about his run during that race at Talladega in 1973. In fact, Isaac was leading the race. But on lap 90, he pulled into pit row, took off his helmet, and quit — not just the Talladega 500, but NASCAR, and auto sports altogether.

Through the years, the story has grown, like stories do. Accounts now read that Isaac heard a "preternatural voice" in his head that made him get out of the race car. That's how ESPN put it in a 2009 story headlined, "They're hearing voices at Talladega." Other stories, like in *The Charlotte Observer* simply say a "voice" played in Isaac's head and told him get out of the car.

Isaac's experience might've been the inspiration for a scene in the 1990 movie *Days of Thunder*. (C'mon. You knew I'd get around to *Days of Thunder*.) In the scene, Cole is tiring to convince Harry to build him another car. But Harry tells him no. Harry says Cole is still spooked.

"Ever since you and Rowdy crashed at Daytona, you've been waiting on something bad to happen to you," Harry tells Cole. "Just like Buddy Bretherton. He started hearing voices. All of them saying one thing: 'Get out of that race car.'"

But to Isaac, the decision wasn't as spooky as all that.

"Something told me to quit. I don't know anything else to do but abide by it," he said. "I wasn't afraid I was going to wreck. I don't have anything to prove to myself or to anybody else. I know how it feels to win and lose. I know how it feels to be a champion. And now I know how it feels to quit."

Isaac claims he did not know about Larry Smith's death at the time of his decision. Coo Coo Marlin hopped in Isaac's car and drove it to finish in 13th place that day.

Remember I told you Issac was impulsive? Well, he returned to NASCAR the very next year and finished 8th in the 1974 Talladega 500.

In that year's 500, came an unsolved mystery that could have been catastrophic — even fatal — to every driver in the field. On the night before the green flag dropped, someone sabotaged 10 cars. Tires were cut in such a way to be unnoticeable. Fan belts, oil lines, and radiator hoses were cut. Sand was funneled into gas tanks.

According to the Racing Reference website, cars belonging

to David Pearson, Bobby Allison, Richard Petty, Donnie Allison, Buddy Baker, Neil Castles, Coo Coo Marlin, Cale Yarborough, Joe Frasson, and James Hylton were sabotaged.

Buddy Baker called it "attempted murder." But the perpetrators never were caught.

The Talladega Curse inspired a 2010 mockumentary-style comedy called *The Legend of Hallowdega*. It was directed by Terry Gilliam (of Monty Python fame) and stars David Arquette with cameos by Dale Earnhardt Jr. and Darrell Waltrip.

In 2009 an ESPN reporter asked Jimmie Johnson — easily the most winningest driver in modern NASCAR — if he believed in the Talladega Curse.

"What's funny is, I tend not to believe in situations like that," Johnsons said. "But then it's always amazing when you find yourself in a moment, and your brain starts freaking out on you, and then all of a sudden you believe that stuff is true."

The Third Man

Consider this portion of T.S. Eliot's famous poem, "The Waste Land:"

"Who is the third who walks always beside you?
When I count, there are only you and I together
But when I look ahead up the white road
There is always another one walking beside you
Gliding wrapt in a brown mantle, hooded
I do not know whether a man or a woman
But who is that on the other side of you?"

Eliot's inspiration for that part of his poem came after he read of Ernest Shackleton's grueling Antarctic expedition in 1916. Shackleton's boat was trapped in ice and he and his team were forced to hike miles over a glacier to survive.

Writing of the journey Shackleton wrote: "I know that during that long and racking march of thirty-six hours over the unnamed mountains and glaciers, it seemed to me often that we were four, not three."

Eliot took a poet's license, changed the four to three and right up to this very day, survival stories will sometimes include what we now call the Third Man Factor or the Third Man Syndrome. In these stories, people say they believe in moments of extreme duress, someone appears to aid in comfort, moral support, or companionship.

Charles Lindbergh claimed someone rode shotgun on his solo trip across the Atlantic. Ron DiFrancesco said he followed such an entity through a wall of flame as he escaped the World Trade Center on 9/11. A pop culture example of the Third Man Factor may be Wilson, the helpful volleyball from the movie *Castaway*. Some simply call these figures guardian angels.

Remember that driver who was convinced someone pulled from his from his flaming car? The Third Man Factor may help to explain it.

The driver was none other than Dale Earnhardt Jr., a driver who — even though he retired — is still probably the most recognized face in all of NASCAR.

In 2004, he was driving a canary-yellow Chevrolet Corvette, taking practice laps before the American Le Mans Series race at Sonoma. He lost control around a turn, his tail end spun out, and he backed into a retaining wall.

That might not have been so bad. But the crash broke the fuel filter and gasoline spilled all over the car, inside and out. The car burst into flame in a great and sudden *woosh!*

An in-car camera caught Earnhardt unbuckling his harness, fire flooding the car all around him. And in a moment he was through the window and out, laying the ground next to the flaming car.

Here's what he said about the crash on his podcast, the *Dale Jr. Download*:

"When I wrecked in the Corvette in 2004 at Sonoma — it caught fire — somebody pulled me out of that car. And I thought that it was a corner worker because I felt somebody put their hands under my armpits and pull me out of the car.

"I didn't get out. I don't have any memory of myself climbing out of the car. And I remember sort of moving like in motion going to lean forward and try to climb out of the car, and then something grabbed me under the armpits, pulled me up over the door bars and then let go of me.

"And I fell to the ground, and there's pictures of me laying on the ground next to the car. I know that when I got to the hospital, I was like, 'Who pulled me out of the car? I gotta say thanks to this person,' because it was a hand! It was physical hands grabbing me! I felt it. And there was nobody there."

But before he told his own story on his own show, Earnhardt talked to Mike Wallace about it on *60 Minutes* just months after the wreck. He told Wallace that he believed his late father helped him out of the car that day.

Even if you're not a race fan, you probably know Dale Earnhardt Sr. He is easily one of the biggest names in NASCAR history. Earnhardt senior died in a three-car crash on the last lap of the 2001 Daytona 500.

"I don't want to put some weird, you know, psycho twist on it like he was pulling me out or anything, but he had a lot to do with me getting out of that car," Earnhardt told Wallace.

8

Past Lives at UVa

"Mama, that's me. I found me."

He wanted to go back home, back to Hollywood. That's where the five-year-old told his mama that his heart exploded.

In his idle time, the boy would yell "action!" and direct imaginary movies in his room. He'd thumb through picture books, remembering stars he'd worked with and some of the movies he'd done.

It was all a curiosity to his parents until the nightmares came. He'd wake screaming in the middle of the night, clutching his chest, replaying the moment he'd had that heart attack.

That's when his mom and dad really began to worry. His dad was a cop and his mom was a court clerk, and both had grown up in traditional Western, Christian households. So, what they were hearing and what it might mean, was squarely outside their raising and their Oklahoma culture.

But their son had begun telling vivid stories. He told them about working with a man named George on the 1932 movie *Night After Night*. He remembered how Rita Hayworth made those drinks, what he called "ice drinks." (They found later that these were actually Coke floats). Then, in an old Hollywood book borrowed from the library, he saw a man in a bowler hat, a black string tie. He pointed to the man and said, eerily, "And, Mama, that's me. I found me."

Children's stories.

What happens when you die? Fear not, I'm not here to evangelize any theory on the topic.

But when a copy of the University of Virginia magazine arrived recently, I found an amazing story I could not put down. It was about a special lab on the campus in Charlottesville, Virginia. There, very serious researchers explore apparitions, near-death experiences, death bed visions, remote viewing, telekinesis, and more.

The lab began, though, with the work of a man who explored peculiar stories told by children. They'd remember things, things they couldn't possibly remember. They'd say things, impossible things.

Sometimes, even marks on their bodies — birthmarks or scars — would match somebody else's. And that somebody else wasn't a relative or a friend or even alive. In some cases, it seemed these children were remembering the lives of people who had passed away.

Researchers at the Division of Perceptual Studies at the University of Virginia have spent years — decades — studying cases of children who say they remember a past life. One of the lead researchers there has a theory about the human soul with at least some support in the spiritual and scientific communities.

Dr. Jim Tucker

Dr. Jim Tucker grew up in North Carolina. In his book, *Return to Life*, he said he and his family attended a Southern Baptist church most Sundays, and "being a dutiful son, I believed what I heard on most Sundays."

Later, he went to college at UNC Chapel Hill. After that, he studied psychiatry at the University of Virginia, what most call UVa for short. While he'd left behind much of the church's dogma, he hadn't reached firm conclusions against spirituality. He was curious, a seeker.

Tucker graduated and set up a private practice in Charlottesville.

He married and his wife opened him up to several spiritual topics like psychics, spirits, and even past lives.

So, Tucker picked up a book by a UVa professor, Ian Stevenson. That book, *Children Who Remember Past Lives*, intrigued Tucker. Later, he'd read in the in *The Charlottesville Daily Progress* that Stevenson's office had won a grant to study the effects of near-death experiences. Finally, his wife convinced him to call Stevenson's office to volunteer. Tucker was quickly invited to the group's next research lunch.

"As I prepared to attend the meeting," Tucker wrote, "I wondered how people who did this kind of work dressed. For instance, did the men wear ties? I decided to go with the most casual work outfit I had, wearing a shirt and tie but not a dressy one. Ian then walked in wearing a three-piece suit."

Tucker began his work with Stevenson with a sort of boring-sounding task. He reviewed the medical records of people who had had near-death experiences, to see how close they'd actually come to death. He said it felt like a "worthwhile but unpaid hobby."

After after two years of this office work, Stevenson invited Tucker into the field. He was researching two cases of children who remembered past lives. The two were soon on an airplane headed for Thailand.

Ampan and Wong

She said her home — her real home — was three miles away in Buhom village. At the time, only a dirt road connected the two villages, and buses rarely ran between the two. The girl's father had a distant relative in Buhom but he'd never been there and no one really ever came from Buhom to their village.

But Ampan told her parents she'd died there. She died in the district hospital of dengue fever, a viral illness spread by mosquitos in tropical and sub-tropical climates. Ampan said she'd died at the hospital and a van took her body away. She ran to catch it but couldn't.

Tucker wrote: "She then began walking and after five miles passed by the road in front of her parents' house. She said she was looking for drinking water. She saw her future mother, and there was a cool breeze. Rather than continue on her journey, she lay down to rest there, and she was subsequently born to her mother."

Ampan said her name — her real name — was Wong or Somwong. She wanted to see her real mother, she said, and she cried for three years to see her. She got her chance. One day her family and her neighbors rented a bus to attend a Buddhist festival in Buhom.

When she got there, Ampan led her mother straight to an unfamiliar home. She ran right up to a woman, hugged her, and called her, mommy. The woman said she did, in fact, have a daughter named Somwong who had died in the way this strange little girl had described it.

In interviews after the event, Tucker — the North-Carolina boy living in Virginia — concluded that "If Ampan was indeed Somwong in a previous life, Somwong's consciousness (or soul or spirit if you like) seems to have remained tightly connected to this realm and to her family."

Paranormal research at UVa?

A question emerges about all of this — well before Ampan, Tucker, the Division of Perceptual Studies, and talks of reincarnation in children. How on earth did a paranormal research laboratory land at on the iconic Southern campus of the University of Virginia?

The school was founded in 1819 by Thomas Jefferson, American president and author of the Declaration of Independence. Jefferson's presence can be felt there today. There's the school's famous student-run honor code, and Jefferson himself laid out the university's original design.

Most notably to that end, look for the towering dome of The

Rotunda, which adorns one end of a sprawling lawn. It's the same kind of dome that caps Monticello, Jefferson's home near the university. It's the same kind of dome that caps the Jefferson Memorial in Washington.

The University of Virginia has flourished since its founding to become a powerhouse. While northeastern kids may dream of going to Harvard or Yale, serious Southern students long for Vanderbilt, William and Mary, Tulane, or the University of Virginia.

UVa is most noted for its programs in business, law, English, medicine, and psychology. And it's an open-minded approach to psychology that allowed Thomas Jefferson's well-loved, well-respected university to become home to a national epicenter of paranormal thought and research.

Dr. Ian Stevenson

Earlier, we met Dr. Ian Stevenson, the man wearing the three-piece suit to that research luncheon Tucker attended. And it's thanks largely to him that the paranormal research center is located at UVa.

Stevenson was born in Canada. And when he was a kid, a case of bronchitis kept him in bed for a spell. It was there Stevenson fell in love with books and learning.

He studied medicine and earned his medical degree. First, he researched biochemistry but really wanted to study the whole person. And there was a question back then that interested him above most others: Why did illness and stress cause one person to have, say, asthma, and in another person illness and stress caused, say, high blood pressure?

He taught later at the Louisiana State University School of Medicine and later studied psychoanalysis at the New Orleans Psychoanalytic Institute. Later, he was named head of UVa's department of psychiatry.

But that question still bugged him. Why do two people have

different physical responses to illness and stress? Stevenson believed that neither nurture nor nature alone — neither heredity nor the environment alone — could accurately account for people's fears, illnesses, or special abilities. Maybe there was a third way. The idea became the foundation of the work Stevenson would build his career upon.

That third way, Stevenson thought, might be a way for some form of personality or memory to be transferred from one person to another. Early in his career, Stevenson was careful about using the "r" word — reincarnation. He had no physical proof that a personality — a soul — could survive death and transfer itself. But reincarnation did become a recurring explanation for what he saw in the cases he followed.

Stevenson worked, traveled, and wrote. His projects won awards at the American Society for Psychical Research and a grant from the Parapsychology Foundation. That grant led Stevenson to India to interview a child who was calming to have past-life memories. He found 25 other cases of past-life memories while he was there. They were the subjects of Stevenson's first book, *Twenty Cases Suggestive of Reincarnation*.

All of it caught the attention of Chester Carlson, the inventor of xerography. What's that? You'll know xerography (and maybe even remember the smell of it) if you ever Xeroxed anything. Carlson, the xerox inventor, gave Stevenson further financial help. This allowed Stevenson to step down as the chair of the psychiatry at UVa and set up his own division, which he called the Division of Personality Studies. Carlson died in 1968 and left the university $1 million for Stevenson's research. That's more than $7 million in today's money.

Stevenson's work earned him the scorn of some of his colleagues and it made the university's administration a bit anxious. But they accepted Carlson's money and that strange, paranormal laboratory was minted on Thomas Jefferson's leafy campus in bucolic Charlottesville, Virginia.

Here's the end of Stevenson's 2007 obituary in the *Washington Post*:

"Dr. Stevenson retired from active research in 2002, leaving his work to successors led by Dr. Bruce Greyson. Dr. Jim Tucker, a child psychiatrist, has carried on Dr. Stevenson's work with children, focusing on North American cases.

"Tucker said that toward the end of his life, Dr. Stevenson had accepted that his long-stated goal of getting science 'to seriously consider reincarnation as a possibility' was not going to be realized in this lifetime.

"But in 1996, no less a luminary than astronomer Carl Sagan, a founding member of a group that set out to debunk unscientific claims, wrote in his book, *The Demon-Haunted World*: 'There are three claims in the [parapsychology] field which, in my opinion, deserve serious study,' the third of which was 'that young children sometimes report details of a previous life, which upon checking turn out to be accurate and which they could not have known about in any other way than reincarnation.'"

The boy from Hollywood

He'd been friends with a cowboy. And that cowboy had this horse and they did tricks together. And the cowboy did commercials for cigarettes. And they'd done a picture together, a movie. And in that movie there was scene that had a closet full of guns. But the cowboy's name was different when they made that movie.

Don't even get him started about trying to talk to Marilyn Monroe one time! She had studio guys all around all the time. But he did try to talk with her at a party once, and one of them fellows punched him right in the eye.

These were the stories that Ryan, a five-year-old kid living in Oklahoma, told his momma and daddy as they thumbed through a Hollywood picture book they'd gotten from the library. He'd kind of always told stories about Hollywood, and the famous people he knew, and the that big house he lived with the swimming pool outside.

But the Hollywood Ryan talked about was an older one, back when Marylin Monroe and Rita Hayworth were leading ladies. It seems if Ryan wanted to make up stories about movies at the time and at his age, he'd maybe string a tale about the Ninja Turtles or the Transformers.

But it wasn't just Hollywood talk with Ryan that made his folks worry. He predicted the future with alarming accuracy. He told his momma about his life when she was pregnant with him. Then there were those nightmares about having a heart attack.

It was all enough for Cyndi, Ryan's mom, to send a "To Whom It May Concern" letter to the Division of Perceptual Studies at the University of Virginia.

Jim Tucker, the man who led the group after Stevenson, received that letter and was immediately intrigued. While most of Stevenson's work focused on cases in Asia, Tucker decided he wanted to focus his work in North America. Ryan's amazing story more than fit the bill.

Ryan and his family agreed to meet Tucker. Before he got there, Cyndi began keeping a journal of Ryan's stories. On a trip to Branson, Missouri, they went to see a patriotic show. During a piece on Pearl Harbor, Ryan became emotional and booed loudly at a clip of Franklin Roosevelt, saying, "Daddy doesn't know what an idiot that man is." He talked about an agency where people changed their names and talked about visiting the Eiffel Tower and China.

Ryan said he was starting to forget his life in Hollywood. That made him sad, he told his mom, but at the same time, he just wanted to be Ryan. His momma looked at him and said that Ryan is a great little boy and that she wanted him to have the answers to the questions he cried about at night.

After Ryan warmed up to Tucker, he told him about Hollywood. During that time, a producer with an A&E show called *The Unexplained* hoped to feature Ryan's case on television. The family agreed, and that bought them a team of researchers who could help find those answers for Ryan.

They dug deep to find the key that could unlock the entire puzzle, and after months, they found it. They found the man Ryan pointed to in that book and said, "That's me momma. I found me."

Though the man in the bowler hat and the string tie was an uncredited extra in the film *Night After Night*, the show's researchers discovered his name was Marty Martyn, who died in 1964. After a series of strenuous tests, Ryan confirmed that he had, indeed, been that man before. The facts that flow and fit together from that breakthrough are nothing less than miraculous.

The film *Night After Night*, which featured Marty Martyn, starred an actor named Gordon Nance. He typically starred in Westerns and did ads for Viceroy cigarettes. Later, the actor changed his name to Wild Bill Elliott.

Stories of Rita Hayworth and Marylin Monroe proved too tough to substantiate. But researchers could prove that Marty Martyn had been a lifelong Republican, which explained why he booed Franklin Roosevelt during that show in Branson.

Ryan talked about an agency where people changed their names. Marty Martyn moved form New York to Los Angeles and began work as an extra and a dance director. But he soon set up shop as a talent agent, the Marty Martyn Agency, which had notable clients like Glenn Ford. If there's ever a place where people change their names, it's a talent agency.

One thing didn't match up, though. Ryan had those nightmares about his heart exploding, a seeming heart attack. Marty Martyn had been a smoker, even had a monogrammed cigarette case. But Martyn died on Christmas Day in 1964 of a cerebral hemorrhage and was in the hospital for leukemia. Martyn died alone, though, and no one witnessed his death.

In the midst of his talk of Hollywood, Ryan told his momma that he'd seen her that night, crying at that restaurant on Daddy's birthday. He watched it from heaven, he said. He knew she was upset because she wanted a little girl.

He said, "This doctor guy did a test and told you I was a boy. You got mad and said he was wrong. You just knew that I was going to be a girl. Mommy, it was Daddy's birthday, you went to a restaurant afterward to eat and you cried for a very long time." It was a hard truth to hear from your child.. But it was the truth, his mother confirmed.

He knew other truths, too. There was his grandmother's first child who had died in childbirth. Even his momma didn't know about that. He told his granny she was going to get chicken pox. She did. He said his grandpa was going to have to buy a new, special wrench. Sure enough, his grandpa said later his wrenches had fallen off the back of his truck.

There were premonitions about broken squirt guns, someone who was going to throw out their back, and Ryan accurately predicted who his second grade teacher was going to be. He was willing to bet his momma an Xbox on it. She didn't take the bet. She was wise not to.

Ryan did finally stop talking about Hollywood. His momma walked in his room one night, after his episode of *The Unexplained* aired on A&E. He'd taken down his movie decorations, his Eiffel Tower, and his pictures of New York.

Tucker said, "He told her it was time to be just a regular kid. He wanted to know if his dad could paint his room and if they could get him some Oklahoma Sooners bedding and sheets. His parents were thrilled."

9

The President and the Honeymooner

A midnight road trip

It was the middle of the night — midnight, as the story goes. It was February, but the air on Key Biscayne, Florida, was warm, around 70 degrees.

The man was in bed and he was tired. He'd played golf, glad-handed, drank, and ate all day at a charity golf event he'd hosted. Among the crowd was his friend, a man he'd referred to as just his "golfing buddy." And they'd played 18 holes together that day.

The man was in a deep sleep when there was a knock on his door. He rose, confused. Maybe he pulled on a robe and tied it across his immense and trademark belly. When he opened the door, he found his friend — his golfing buddy — standing there.

The man himself — the one in the night robe — was an international star. But his friend was easily one of the most recognizable men on the planet. It surprised the man that his golfing buddy was there at all and at that late hour. But what struck him the most was that he was all alone.

When the two played the 15th hole earlier that day, the conversation turned to UFOs, a subject in which both had immense interest. But they'd left the topic on the golf course.

Standing in his doorway, the man's friend beckoned him to get dressed and get in his car. He had something — something only that friend among all others in the entire country — could show him.

Florida is Southern

Some might argue that Florida ain't Southern. Try telling that to Lynyrd Skynyrd fans. Also, go grab a beer at the Flora-Bama and then tell me Florida ain't Southern.

But, yeah, you'll argue that's northern Florida and the panhandle. Head south and Florida's its own deal. I get that.

But southern Florida is so wild and so beautiful and so diverse that someone has to claim it. So, I — here and now, by the power vested in me by Mystery, the Haint Blues mule — formally claim Florida for the South. Done and done.

Even so, Key Biscayne (or any kind of Key in general) will sound like an exotic place to the average fan of the Charlie Daniels Band. And from what I've heard in Jimmy Buffett songs, the Florida Keys are whole other worlds, separate from mainland USA.

But Key Biscayne is only the starting point in this story of a most mysterious meet-up. The characters in our story are men you know, with catchphrases almost as famous as they are. The two of them light out from the Keys and end up in another world entirely. And a glimpse into that world leaves one man shaken, and the other with tears in his eyes, if you believe the stories.

And that brings me to an important note. The stories in this book are real. That doesn't make them true. These stories live in newspapers, books, interviews, oral traditions, and memories. The tales in this book exist somewhere out there; I haven't made them up. But I also can't prove them to be true. I'm not trying to, and I don't want to. Telling these stories is important because they are a part of Southern culture, of who we are.

To me, the Gray Man and the Bell Witch are just as relevant to Southern culture as bluegrass and biscuits and gravy. I like to go out to the fringe, find these stories, and explore them. And I love to write them down and report them to you.

Skeptics and even paranormal researchers scoff at this road-trip story. But I think you should still hear it. It's never been proven, but it's never been disproven either. Even snopes.com has a big, old question mark on it. Either way, the story is a ton of fun, a Southern road trip with two famous buddies heading out — just the two of them — in the middle of the night to parts unknown.

Alright, let's load up with the President and the Honeymooner and head out to southern Florida. We're looking for real-world evidence of UFOs, aliens, and massive government conspiracy to cover it all up.

A worried wife

They were still married but they were separated. Things had settled down and things were looking up. That's when she gave an interview with *Esquire* magazine. She was writing a book about her life, about living with her famous husband. And Beverly McKittrick was looking to gin up some press about it. In doing so, she maybe said more than she should have.

She told the magazine writer that her husband had come home late one night and she was worried. When he got home, he looked haggard. After some questions, her husband told her he'd been to what was then called Homestead Air Force Base, about an hour away.

His friend, he said, had taken him there to show him the bodies of aliens. He said they were "only about two feet tall, with bald heads and disproportionately large ears."

The man couldn't get many answers about the outing from his friend. And that friend surely did have or could get the answers. But the man suspected a spacecraft must have crashed somewhere nearby.

Whatever it was and whatever he saw that night, Beverly said her husband, Jackie Gleason, went on to talk about the events of that night all the next day.

The Honeymooner

Jackie Gleason was a funnyman. He was a comedian, actor, and writer. His best known character was Ralph Kramden, the brash New York City bus driver, in the 1950s television hit comedy called *The Honeymooners*.

Gleason went on to host his own variety show, the aptly named *Jackie Gleason Show*, through the '50s and '70s. The filming of that show moved at some point from New York to Miami, which helps explain how Gleason got to that home on Key Biscayne.

But after Ralph Kramden, most people know Gleason from his role as Buford T. Justice in the *Smokey and the Bandit* films. Justice was the foul-mouthed Texas sheriff from Montague County, chasing the Bandit all over the South.

Now, Bandit and the Snowman were trying to illegally transport 400 cases of Coors from Texarkana to Atlanta. But Sheriff Justice wanted to get them mainly because Bandit had absconded with his son Junior's fiancee. And, as films go, it don't get much more Southern than *Smokey and the Bandit*.

But Gleason — in real life — was particularly interested in the paranormal, particularly UFOs and aliens.

For proof, look to the house Gleason built in Peekskill, New York. It sat on six acres CBS gave him in addition to his salary and royalties. He called it Round Rock Hill. It was recently on the market. Here's how *Parade* magazine described it:

"The unique, round structure has no right angles, and along with the guest house there are five bedrooms, six baths, a library, an entertainment space, a curved kitchen and more.

"An incredible curved marble stairway leads to the upper level, and huge windows give the entire home a light, airy feel."

That "round structure" looks just like a UFO. Consider that he called the main house the "Mother Ship" and the rounded guest house the "Scout Ship."

Further proof of Gleason's interest in the paranormal is plain. When he passed, he left his collection of books to the University of Miami.

According to the school, the collection includes "1,700 volumes of books, journals, proceedings, pamphlets, and publications" all mainly about the paranormal.

"It includes materials on such topics as: witchcraft, folklore, extrasensory perception (ESP), unidentified flying objects (UFOs), reincarnation, mysticism, spiritualism, mental telepathy, the occult, ghosts, clairvoyance, cosmology, demons, hypnosis, life after death, mediums, psychical research, voodooism, and others."

The dead little men

Gleason apparently chided his then-wife Beverly McKittrick for disclosing his UFO night out with his friend that night back in 1974. The interview she gave soured their relationship, she said, and ended in their divorce. She never wrote that book she was working on.

"I just made that one statement about the UFOs and it appeared in *Esquire* and I guess a few other places and he didn't like that and I thought, I just can't go through with this," McKittrick said. "Let him live his life. So, I never wrote the book."

No book, but she did give an interview with UFO researcher Kenny Young much later on. In it, she gave him the highlights of Gleason's midnight road trip.

"He and Nixon were in contact quite a bit and I'm not sure how that was arranged, but it seems that their meetings were set up by an associate of Nixon's," she told Young. "After he got back, he was very pleased he had an opportunity to see the dead little men in cases. He explained to me what they looked like and he was still talking about it the next day."

Gleason and the President

Jackie Gleason was a supporter of the Republican Party and through that support he had developed a relationship with President Richard Nixon. Google around and it's easy to find pictures of the two of them on the golf course.

It's said that Nixon was privately fascinated with the idea of UFOs. There is also a well-known conspiracy theory that Nixon wrote a letter disclosing the entire alien/human relationship and hid it somewhere in the White House. As the conspiracy theory goes, that letter is to be revealed at a time in the future prescribed by Nixon and it is to be read aloud to senior advisors and the press.

As far as the Gleason/Nixon road trip, I've relied on the best evidence available: an alleged transcript from an alleged interview. It's apparently the story Gleason told to UFO researcher Larry Warren. Warren was a witness to the Rendlesham Forest UFO incident.

If that doesn't sound familiar, Rendlesham Forest is considered Britain's Roswell. If Roswell doesn't sound familiar, invite me over for biscuits and gravy and I'll tell you all about it. (Man, this guy sure does talk about biscuits and gravy a whole lot, doesn't he?)

According to Warren's story, Gleason invited him to his UFO house in New York. And, after several drinks, Gleason told him this story:

"I want to tell you something, which in any case will come out one day. We have got them [extraterrestrial beings].

"It was back when Nixon was in office that something truly amazing happened to me. We were close golfing buddies and had been out on the golf course all day when somewhere around the 15th hole, the subject of UFOs came up.

"Not many people know this but the president shares my interests in this matter and has a large collection of books in his home on UFOs just like I do.

"For some reason, however, he never really took me into confidence about what he personally knows to be true. ...one of the reasons being that he was usually surrounded by so many aides and advisors.

"Later that night, matters changed radically. Richard Nixon showed up at my house around midnight. He was all alone for a change. There were no secret agents with him or anyone else. I said, 'Mr. President, what are you doing here?' And he said he wanted take me someplace and show me something.

"I got into the president's private car and we sped off into the darkness. Our destination, I found on arrival, was Homestead Air Force Base.

"I remember we got to the gate and this young MP came up to the car to look to see inside and his jaw seemed to drop a foot when he saw who was behind the wheel. He just sort of pointed and we headed off.

"We drove to the very far end of the base in a segregated area, finally stopped near a well-guarded building. The security police saw us coming and just sort of moved back as we passed them and entered the structure.

"There were a number of labs we passed through first before we entered a section where Nixon pointed our what he said was the wreckage from a flying saucer, enclosed in several large cases.

"Next we went into an inner chamber and there were six or eight of what looked like glass-topped Coke freezers. Inside them were the mangled remains of what I took to be children. Then, upon close examination, I saw some of the other figures looked quite old. Most of them were terribly mangled as if they had been in an accident.

"All in all it was a very pathetic sight. At one point, the president had tears in his eyes and, finally, I realized that this was not his way of trying to be humorous."

Nixon, Gleason, and UFOs forever

Now, Gleason denied this story every time he was asked about it.

He passed away in 1987 and he never, ever admitted to seeing alien bodies in a Coke cooler with Richard Nixon.

The best evidence paranormal researchers can point to for any veracity in the tale is the fact that Nixon often did try to skirt his Secret Service detail. The truth of the rest of the story lies with Beverly McKittrick.

After she told it to *Esquire*, she wondered about the story, too. Only because Gleason got so mad about her telling it. She wondered if he got mad because she was spreading some story he'd made up, maybe a cover for staying out late. (I wonder how far I could get away with something by telling my wife that I was out late because the president was showing me some alien bodies?)

No matter what you think of the story, the two men are passed and the truth is no longer out there. But the story remains, and it will resurface anytime anyone Googles any combination of Jackie Gleason, Richard Nixon, and UFOs.

10

The Lizard Man

"I was sheriff during the time the Lizard Man made his appearance in Lee County. It was during the year of 1988.

"I took this very serious because if we turned our backs on it and said they wasn't nothing to it... Well, if it attacks someone's children or even adults, I wouldn't've just had to leave Lee County I'd've had to leave the state." — Lee County Sheriff Liston Truesdale 1988

A late-night ride through the swamp

Even though his windows were down, his car smelled like french fries. That's because he smelled like french fries. But that was same as ever for 17-year-old Chris Davis and it didn't matter. He'd punched out of McDonald's and was free as a bird.

He was driving. And the breeze was blowing in on him as he was on his way home, home to Browntown just outside of Bishopville. If you've never worked a late-night shift somewhere, you might not know the serenity and unique joy of *ending* a late-night shift somewhere. But I bet Chris Davis did.

Davis' car was aimed for home. At the moment, he was on a long, lonely stretch of backroad. But a solitary drive home didn't scare Davis, not even driving through the creepy Scape Ore Swamp, not even at 2 a.m. He'd driven that stretch outside of Bishopville a hundred times, and his high-beams cut back that South Carolina darkness and showed his way home.

If there was anything out there, that was fine. Chris Davis was inside and wouldn't get out until...*pop!*

Monsters among us

Monsters live among us. No, Bigfoot probably doesn't work in the cubicle next door. Nessie probably don't swim at your same YMCA. Monsters live in our collective conscience — in our myths and legends.

Now, you can choose to believe or disbelieve a myth or a legend. Sometimes you can't choose monsters. A lot of time it's monsters that'll creep into your head if you ever find yourself alone in the woods at night. Sometimes it's monsters that flood you with fear when something touches your leg in the deep part of the lake.

They're out there, I think. Some of them, anyway. But that monsters are in our heads? There's no doubt. And that's just how I like it. From where I sit, I see Southern monsters aplenty. But there's few of them as unique, modern, and well documented as the one that popped out of a South Carolina swamp in the 1980s.

A terrifying encounter

Nothing, and I mean nothing, can pop a bubble of joy and serenity like flat tire. That's just what 17-year-old Chris Davis had when he was driving through Scape Ore Swamp all alone late on that July night back in 1988. One moment he was cruising along, maybe with his arm propped up on his window rolled down, the breeze blowing in, and maybe some music playing low on the radio. Then, *pop!*

When you get a flat, your whole mind resets. Your daydreams evaporate in a sudden poof. But once you've slowed and finally stopped, your mind eases off the break pedal of survival and then reality washes right over you like cold molasses. You have to fix a flat.

Chris Davis was almost home. He was tired. And it was awfully dark out there and him all by himself. Now, before getting home, getting a shower, and settling in for some hard-earned rest and relaxation, Davis was going to have to fix that flat tire, out there in the wet heat, kneeling around on that dusty dirt road.

"After I finished changing it, I was putting the flat and the jack in the trunk," Davis told police later. "I looked back and I saw red eyes...big red eyes and a thing running towards me from those trees and it was kicking up drifts of dust as it went.

"I jumped in the driver's side and as I was shutting the door, he grabbed the door. So, I jerked the door shut and pulled off. I look in the mirror and I saw a big image and a loud crash on top of the car."

That's what Davis said in a 1988 interview, right after his encounter with what would become the Lizard Man of Scape Ore Swamp. He said the creature was tall and black-green and wet. And the thing chased him up to 35 miles an hour and finally jumped on top of the car. But Davis was finally able to throw the thing off the top of the car.

He told Lee County Sheriff Liston Truesdale, "It was strong and it wasn't an animal and it wasn't a man." Davis said when he finally got home that night, the top of his car had been all scratched up and it was wet.

"I said OK, draw it," the sheriff said of his interview with Davis after the chase. "He drew it immediately."

Davis drew a tall human figure with a small head and two large eyes. Two long arms spindle down beside a meaty torso. The arms end in three fingers, each with a long claw. He said it was about seven feet tall, stood on two legs, and those eyes, of course, were big and red.

The town and the swamp

Bishopville, South Carolina sits right in the middle of the state. It's almost halfway between Columbia and Florence on highway 15 just off interstate 20. Beautiful old homes dot the landscape of the town and Wikipedia calls Pearl Fryer's Topiary Gardens "one of the most breath-taking attractions in South Carolina." Bishopville's iconic water tower looms above the town of about 3,500 souls.

The Scape Ore Swamp lies southwest of town. Its main channel of murky, dark water stays full all year long, It runs through low hills of matted underbrush and thick woods. The name Scape Ore came as it was the general location of an escaped, uh, trollop running from volunteers in the Revolutionary War.

But there is no doubt that Chris Davis' wild encounter put Bishopville and Scape Ore Swamp on the map, as they say. And sightings of the Lizard Man didn't stop with that young man who got a flat tire.

That wild summer

In the wee hours of a Sunday morning, Lee County Sheriff's deputy Wayne Atkinsons and South Carolina state trooper Mike Hodge were called out Scape Ore Swamp to investigate a Bigfoot sighting. The two took the call seriously, and within an hour, they were beaming their flashlights along the rough banks of the swamp.

Here's how the *Time and Democrat* newspaper described their search:

"Less than hour later and about one mile away, the two officers stumbled upon some tracks — fresh, big tracks. And they believe whatever is out there watched as they stepped out of the trooper's car to investigate garbage strewn onto the dirt road.

"They also examined two battered cardboard trash bins and a broken tree limb dangling about nine feet overhead before they got back in the car, drove on down the road and turned around.

"When they returned to the site, they found that something had walked across their tire tracks, leaving a fresh set of three-toed, 14-by-7 inch prints before it entered the woods.

"If it was a prankster, how would they know someone would

come down that road," said Atkinson, a 10-year veteran of the Lee County Sheriff's Department.

"I'm convinced there was something out there," said Hodge, a former Marine who had been with the patrol for a year and a half. "If a prankster was out there and the law pulled up, they would have gotten out of there."

The week before this, Sheriff Truesdale was called out to the home of Tom and Mary Waye. They woke one Friday morning to find their car in the driveway had been chewed up. The sheriff checked around the house for tracks and found some. But he said what he found did not belong to a cow or a deer. He thought they might've been bear tracks.

It was enough for the sheriff to call in Matt Knox, a biologist with the South Carolina Wildlife and Marine Resources Department. He said the tracks he found and short hairs he found on the chrome and molding of the car belonged probably to a red fox but sent samples off to the University of Georgia.

Knox also interviewed Chris Davis, the young man with the harrowing encounter with the creature. Knox concluded there was no Lizard Man.

"As far as I'm concerned, it's no wild animal. All I can guess, it was a man, possibly a drunk" who had been lying in a muddy, wet ditch and was trying to catch a ride with Davis.

Whatever it was mucking around out there in Scape Ore Swamp, Bishopville went wild for it.

Associated Press July 21, 1988

BROWNTOWN — Traffic has been heavy at Scape Ore Swamp in Lee County since first one, then several sightings of a so-called "Lizard Man" have come pouring in.

"This is the most excitement we've had in a long time," Tony White said as he and three other friends set off to find the monster and collect a $1 million bounty offered by Columbia radio station WCOS for the creature's capture.

Associated Press August 9, 1988

Bishopville, South Carolina — Visitors have been pulling off Interstate 20 for the past few weeks to satisfy their curiosity about the Lizard Man.

Marina Watson of the local Chamber of Commerce said business has been brisk this summer, but had no estimate of how much money Lizardmania has put into the local economy.

If it's Lizard Man paraphernalia you're after, there are hats, T-shirts, inflatable toy dinosaurs, and even wanted posters with an artist's impression of the Lizard Man.

This story said a can of Liz-A-Rid repellent sat on Sheriff Truesdale's desk.

Boston Globe — August 30, 1988.

Bishopville, S.C. — As Jerry Rooks like to tell it, Lizard Man is the biggest event in Lee County in 125 years.

"This is the biggest thing that's happened here since the Civil War," said Rooks who owns Rook's Sales and Service, a general store in the county seat, Bishopville.

A tall, inflatable lizard — testimony to the creature a 17-year-old boy said chased him near a swamp — stands in Rooks' storefront under a sign saying, "Lizard Man Country."

Later, Sheriff Truesdale said, "At that time when all of this first broke, it went all over the world in three days time. I got calls from all over the world. One of the things the media has done was, they'd take it from Chris Davis and that was all. But this thing, at least 12 people saw it that summer."

Frank Mitchell was one of those people. He was a crop duster, covering the thousands of acres of the local cotton farms. One morning, he loaded up for a day in the cockpit, fired up his engine, and pointed his small plane down a long grassy strip that served as his runway.

"There's a point down there that if you're not off the ground, you'd better throttle back and stop," Mitchell said. "After that point, you'd better hope you fly.

"That's about where I was when I saw this...whatever it was...crossed the runway in front of me. He turned his head and looked at the plane and kept on. The thing had a kind of lope in its walk. Much taller than you. I'd guess it it was eight and a half, nine feet tall."

Lizardmania continued around Bishopville that summer of 1988. Many more came forward to say they'd seen the Lizard Man.

That summer, a Bigfoot researcher headed to Bishopville and concluded that it wasn't a Lizard Man at all but a Skunk Ape, the famous Bigfoot-like creature from Florida. Another man claimed he was driving around in a camouflaged car, looking for the creature. He said he found him and claimed to shoot Lizard Man the neck. Later, though, he claimed the story was all a hoax "to keep the legend alive."

Chris Davis had to quit his job at McDonald's that summer. He was picked up by three agents who whisked the teen around the state. They'd booked him on radio shows and television shows. They had him signing autographs and T-shirts at local malls. That all slowed as the summer turned to autumn and Davis entered his junior year of school. But his weekends were booked solid for three months.

It all became so much that sheriff Truesdale said he wished the whole thing would go away. And eventually it did. But Bishopville remembers.

Lizard Man returns

In 2015, a new spate of Lizard Man sightings once again brought attention to Scape Ore Swamp.

In August of that year, Jim Wilson told Columbia's *The State* newspaper that "something came out of the woods and crossed the Scape Ore Bridge." He said it "was a tall, dark figure that had a tail and appeared to have scales. ... It was almost like an alligator with a short nose and long legs." Wilson said the creature turned toward him and quickly ran back down into the water. He got back into his car and was able to get one last glimpse of the creature as it crossed the swamp.

A woman — Mary — told the newspaper that while she would not give her last name, that she and a friend saw Lizard Man after church one Sunday.

"We saw Lizard Man come out of the woods and run along the tree line," she said. "My hand to God, I am not making this up."

Lizard Man has kept state and local wildlife and law enforcement officials busy since 1988. They often get calls attributed to the creature. They turn out to be nothing, more often than not, they say. But they always respond.

Officials, too, have speculated about what Lizard Man may have actually been. One politician thought a man back in 1988 dressed up as Lizard Man and scared people but that the person had probably passed away, taking the truth with him. A biologist explained the tracks could have been from an escaped ostrich or emu.

If you want to see Lizard Man for yourself, head to Bishopville in June. There, you'll find the Lizard Man Festival. It's held right there at the Cotton Museum on Cedar Lane.

The first event in 2018 featured panels of cryptozoologists like Lyle Blackburn who wrote *Lizard Man: the True Story of the Bishopville Monster*. The event also featured tours of the Scape Ore Swamp and, of course, a selfie station with a life-size Lizard Man stand in.

11

Ghost Gumbo Part 2

The most famous ghost in Memphis

The little girl was maybe 12 or 13, and she was elated. It was the 1920s, and the mood in Downtown Memphis was absolutely electric. And the little girl was right in the middle of it all, dressed in her finest white dress and black stockings.

Maybe the girl and her parents had been shopping at Goldsmith's or Lowenstein's, those massive department stores up on Main Street. Or, maybe, they were on their way to see show at the elegant Orpheum Theatre, sometimes back then called the South's Finest Theater.

Either way, that's right where they ended up, looking up at the twinkling lights and marquee of that magnificent old playhouse right on the corner of Main Street and Beale Street.

But you had to step carefully at that corner. A trolley line ran right there. Those massive trolleys lumbered and dinged right in front of the old playhouse, carrying folks up and down Main Street.

Horror quickly broke the spell of that enchanting scene. The little girl's parents screamed. The crowd around them gasped. The little girl, dressed in her city best, stepped right onto those tracks and right in front of one of those enormous lumbering trolleys.

In a flash, someone scooped up the little girl and began running for the first door they saw. Inside the lobby of the Orpheum Theatre, those bystanders found there was little they could do for that little girl. She died under the vaulted ceilings of that grand old theater.

But some say she loves the Orpheum, yes, loves it to this day. Because for the last 80 years or so, that's just where that little girl has stayed.

It had been a wonderful show back in the early 1970s, but it was over. The crowd was leaving the gorgeous Orpheum Theatre in Downtown Memphis. But a few stayed.

They were friends of Vincent Astor, the Orpheum's manager. He invited them to stay after the show and come down to the side of the beautiful stage under the theater's magnificent vaulted ceiling.

Astor was going to play Orpheum's grand organ for them. It's a massive antique Wurlitzer that looks like a whimsical circus car. Astor sat and began playing softly at the rows of keyboards and foot pedals. The organ pumped on in peaceful serenity, but the spell was suddenly broken.

"Somebody said, who's that?" Astor said. "They said they saw a little girl dressed all in white, playing in the lobby."

By the time Astor and his friends were listening to the organ, tales of a tiny, playful spirit had begun to resurface at the Orpheum. Folks were seeing a little girl in white playing all over the massive theater.

"She was described as girl of about 12 years old with long dark braids in a white, short dress with black stockings but no shoes," Astor said.

The little girl would come around when Astor would play soft songs on the organ, children's songs, especially. He could almost guarantee a ghostly encounter if he played "Never, Never Land" from *Peter Pan*.

But it wasn't only Astor and his friends who saw the spirit. It's been said that Yul Brenner saw a little girl in the Orpheum's mezzanine while he rehearsed *The King and I*. A group of actors from New York arrived at the Orpheum for a production of *Fiddler on the Roof*. They quickly heard the story of the little ghost girl that haunted the theater. Being a bit superstitious, the troupe organized a seance in the balcony before their first performance, in an effort to appease her.

The spirt got a name in the early 1970s. A University of Memphis parapsychology professor had heard the stories of the ghost. Dr. Lee Sutter brought in his class and a Ouija board to the theater and they all set to work on stage.

The professor and his students gathered around the board, hands placed gently on the planchette. While they focused their energy, Astor played his organ softly, off the side of the stage.

Somewhere in those hushed, haunting moments, they connected. Sutter and his group of students began communicating with a spirit, the spirit of a little girl. She told them she was the one who had been seen in the theater for all of those years. She said she was 12. She said she died in 1921. She said her name was Mary.

Mary had been seen so often in the Orpheum, that folks even knew where she'd be. She likes to sit in seat C-5, Box 5 on the mezzanine level. That's where countless actors, audience members, and Orpheum employees have seen Mary over the years.

"Although her blank stare and ethereal appearance have upset some who have seen her, the little girl known as Mary has never disrupted a performance," the Orpheum said in a Facebook post. "In fact, it seems as though she adores the theatre."

Mary is Memphis' most-famous ghost. She's one of the most famous ghosts in Tennessee, second only to that strange spirit known as the Bell Witch.

Though many have seen Mary, not much is known about her, not even her death. The story about the trolley is the most-told version.

But some have suggested she fell or was burned in the fire of the original Orpheum building in 1923.

The most famous ghost in Florida
She comes out at night
In the moon and starlight
You know she's buried just over the ridge
And she sing her sad songs
To her lover long gone
Each night at the Bellamy Bridge
— Ghost of Bellamy Bridge (Ernest Toole, 2015)

It was like a Southern fairy tale. She was young and beautiful. He was young and successful. They fell madly in love and got married. But the fairy tale ended in a tragedy, a horror, and a haunting that spans two centuries.

In the early 1800s, Elizabeth Croom met Samuel Bellamy in North Carolina. They were both children of the so-called "planting aristocracy." That just means their families were rich farmers.

They decided to get married and move to Florida. And, being a rich kid and a rich doctor, Samuel built Elizabeth a mansion there as a wedding gift. She was so taken with the home that she requested that the two marry right there in the mansion's rose garden.

It was a sweltering May day in Florida, but it hardly mattered. The bride looked so beautiful in her tailored white wedding gown and gossamer veil. And a line she added to the end of her vows moved many to tears. She looked Samuel in the eyes and said, "I will love you always and forever. Never will I leave you."

As they dried their eyes, the guests moved into the mansion for a grand wedding reception filled with music, dancing, wedding cake, and unending bottles of Madeira and champagne.

All the furniture in the "big room" had been moved away for a grand ball. The sun was low, so candles and lamps were lit.

The room hushed. In that flickering light, all eyes fell on the bride for the couple's first dance. Elizabeth and Samuel started the waltz and moved and swayed fluidly around the room.

As they whirled, Elizabeth's long, gossamer veil swung back from her head. I bet she and the whole scene looked so beautiful. But that's the moment tragedy struck.

Her veil licked over a candle flame. The flame hungrily consumed that airy fabric. Then Elizabeth's hair was on fire, and then her dress, and soon the beautiful young bride was completely engulfed in flame.

Screaming in a frenzied panic, Elizabeth ran from the room, out the front door, across the veranda, down the wide steps of the mansion and out into the yard.

The crowd gaped at the scene in disbelief. They all stood motionless for one moment until Samuel and his brother gathered up a rug and ran after Elizabeth in the yard. They threw the rug on her, wallowed her to the ground, and smothered the flames.

Elizabeth moaned inside the rug amid the smell of flame, and smoke and singed hair. But she was still alive. The brothers carried her upstairs to what would have been her wedding bed.

There, they began cutting away the burned pieces of her white wedding dress and rubbing lard on the burns that covered most of her body. They nursed Elizabeth until Samuel saw the end was near. He sent his brother away for a private last few moments with his brand-new bride.

The next day, the community turned out for Elizabeth's funeral at nearby Bellamy Plantation. She was buried in a grove of live oaks. Elizabeth was 18 years old.

Samuel mourned his wife in a black mood that some said bordered on madness. Time passed. He took a new job. He was even elected to public office. Still, though, he would not enter the home where Elizabeth died. He did not want to see the remains of the fire that consumed his bride. But he wouldn't let the home be changed, either.

Hurricanes and yellow fever came. So did financial woes, family squabbles, and the Seminole War. To soothe those troubled times, Samuel took to drinking, sometimes entirely too much. Three days after Christmas in 1853, Samuel rode down to the ferry landing in Chattahoochee. There, he slit his own throat with a straight razor.

It was after his death, that some say Elizabeth rose from her grave to keep that wedding vow that moved so many to tears all those years ago. "I will love you always and forever. Never will I leave you."

It's said that Elizabeth roams the swamps and creeks near the Chipola River, especially near an old, abandoned bridge. And she's been seen there since the 1800s. In 1890, a story in a local newspaper carried the headline, "The lady of the Bellamy Bridge has been seen of late."

Reports in the late 1800s and early 1900s had Elizabeth as an angry and vengeful spirit. Her wrath was so well known, that folks wouldn't cross Bellamy Bridge at night, or did so by taking their lives in their own hands.

Later, though, it seems Elizabeth cooled. Modern visitors to the bridge describe cold spots, a mysterious fog, and feelings of sadness and dread. Some have even caught odd lights and mists in photographs.

If you want to see for yourself, hit the Bellamy Bridge Heritage Trail. Head down route 162, just west of the Chipola River north of Marianna. There, you can walk a half-mile-long trail that ends at the now-defunct Bellamy Bridge.

Walk in after dark. See if you can catch a glimpse of the ghost of Bellamy Bridge, Florida's most well-known ghost story.

Chloe and the Myrtles Plantation
She had a plan. She was going to bake a cake.

This cake was going have a special ingredient, one that would help secure her place in the house and keep her out of the sweltering, semi-tropical heat of the indigo fields. This cake, she might've believed, was one that would save her life.

But it did not. It did quite the opposite. But that young lady's cake and its special ingredient — oleander, if you believe the tales — sparked one of the most-told ghost stories of the great state of Louisiana, if not the entire South.

St. Francisville, Louisiana, is the seat of tiny St. Feliciana Parish. If Louisiana is a boot, St. Francisville is the instep. Anyway, it's just north of Baton Rouge.

Drive Highway 61 through there. You'll find cafes, a hospital, dollar stores, and all the rest you'd imagine to find in small-town USA. But turn west off the highway right there at the Gas Lane station, and you'll find the Myrtles Plantation, the "Home of Mystery and Intrigue" as the sign reads.

Turn down that little road, through the white picket-fence gate, and that gritty small town melts away. Live oaks drip with Spanish moss over a sun-dappled lane.

At the end, sits the beautiful Creole-style cottage. Its wide and long with five gables along the roof, just like many plantation houses there in the 19th century.

The Myrtles, though, boasts a 125-foot-wide veranda that wraps around the entire southern portion of the home, perfect for lazy days of rocking chairs and sipping sweet tea. There, you'll find the scrollwork, shutters, window frames, doors and, yes, even the porch ceiling painted a particular shade of light blue. It's most definitely a haint blue.

Throughout the house there's ornamental ironwork, stained glass, exotic tapestries, a crystal chandelier, marble mantels, and gold-leaf furnishings from France. In short, it seems a model of antebellum Southern charm.

But that Southern charm came at a dreadful price. The home and its fancy ironwork and French furniture and all was built on the backs of slave labor. Men and women were stolen from their homes, chained, and shipped across the sea. In America, they were bought and sold as human livestock, forced to work on big farms all over the country, just like the Myrtles Plantation.

There, the slaves tended to large fields of indigo, a huge crop in the 1800s, used as a dye for fabrics. The work was mundane, back-breaking, and unbearable in that muggy Louisiana heat.

Chloe was an enslaved person, though she had never worked those fields. But she knew those that did and had seen their spirits and their bodies broken. She worked in the house, taking care of Judge Clark Woodruff and his family.

As the story goes, the judge and Chloe had an "affair." And I'll put "affair" in quotation marks. I don't pretend to know what went on, but if the judge wanted Chloe, there probably wasn't much she could do about it.

Anyhow, as the story goes, the judge began an "affair" with another enslaved girl in the house. Chloe worried. What if this complicated things between her and the judge? Or even that other girl? Maybe that other girl could say she wanted Chloe out of the house? What then? Would she be forced out of doors, into the fields with the heat, and mosquitos, and endless labor? Would she, too, find her spirit and body broken like the rest?

No. She wouldn't let that happen. She needed a plan, one that played to her unique position in the house. In the end, she decided she needed to bake a cake, a very special cake.

In the kitchen, she mixed the flour and sugar and eggs and milk. Maybe she looked up from the mixing bowl and looked around the room, turning all the way around to make sure she was alone.

Then, and only then, would she reach into her apron and pull out, maybe, a small cloth pouch. She opened it and paused. Should she do this? Is this the way, the way to save her own life? Was the risk too great? She decided it was the only way and the risk was measured. She knew how much oleander would make someone sick, not kill them.

She'd bake her cake and serve it to the judge's daughters. They'd get sick and call for Chloe, their beloved Chloe. She'd just have to stay in and nurse them back to health. Once the judge saw how well she did, he'd just have to let her stay in the house. With the risk and reward balanced in her mind, Chloe turned that cloth pouch over the mixing bowl and laced that batter with those poisonous oleander leaves.

It sealed her fate and those of the the judge's daughters. Chloe used too much. Those little girls died.

Turns out, too, that Chloe wasn't as sneaky as she thought in the kitchen that day. Word had gotten around to the other slaves and they were worried. What if the judge thought they were in on it? They'd be sent to the fields or worse, killed.

Fearing guilt by association, the other slaves in the house dragged Chloe from her bed that night, hanged her from a tree, and threw her body in the nearby Bayou Sara. That's the story anyway.

But many say Chloe returned to the Myrtles and remains on the grounds to this day. Her apparition has been seen so many times by house workers that it's become a sort of routine. Visitors travel far and wide to catch a glimpse of the ghost. Many say she wears a green turban. Footsteps are heard all over the house. Misty handprints appear on the windows for no reason.

In 1992, an insurance man was at the Myrtles taking photographs for his company. When the film was developed, he spotted someone in a photograph he was sure was not there when he took it.

Standing there in the breezeway between the General's Store and the Butler's Pantry, appeared to be a woman, wearing a headdress of some kind, maybe a turban. But something was odd about her. The white clapboard siding was clearly visible through parts of her body.

Visit Myrtle's Plantation today and you can buy this photograph. It's on a famous postcard, called, simply, the Chloe Postcard.

12

Old-Timey Bigfoot

A grim prediction (and predictor)

It was November but, by god, it was hot. The man and his friend were slashing and hacking their way through tangles of scrub and underbrush in this untamed land. Sweat ran in streams down the man's back and down his arms as he brought his blade up over his head and back down again at some vine or bush as he pushed forward.

The going was slow, to be sure, and it gave the man a lot of time to think. He was between two worlds. He was a living legend in the world he was leaving behind. Revered in his own time for his accomplishments. Loved by all as a living folk hero who loomed large in the national imagination for taming the wilds around him with superhuman abilities, a fair mind, and his trademark grin.

But he felt rejected by that world. And he still felt the sting of it all every time he slashed, cracking the trail before him bit by bit.

The fight on that trail was worth it, he thought. Because at the end of it, lay a land of opportunity. Unspoiled lands just waited for claim, and their wildness just called out for someone just like him to tame them. He'd left his family behind, but he planned to call for them when he settled in and staked his claim in the new world he was so wiling to fight for.

He doubted he could go back to his old life even if he wanted to. He'd burned that bridge in Memphis. He'd been madder than a wet hornet. But as he hacked, he might have thought, lordy, did I really say that...out loud to a room full important people? But then again maybe not. Uncertainty and self doubt weren't really in this man's bailiwick.

But the man was also happy. He was out of doors again, cutting through rough territory that had been largely unexplored. It was the same kind of work on the same kind of adventure that had brought him that national recognition. And he was back at it, away from the cultured crowds of Nashville and Washington. The sun was on his face again.

But the mental and physical strain — and that dad-gum heat — finally settled on the man. So he stopped for a rest. But almost as soon as he sat down, he got a dire warning. Turn around. Go back home. Peril and death lay before you. And, if you believe a letter this revered statesman and folk hero wrote his brother-in-law during that trip, that warning came from a tall, hairy beast standing on two legs at about 7 or 8 feet tall.

Establishing Bigfoot

It seems most folks believe Bigfoot was "discovered" or "invented" (depending on your beliefs I guess) in America around the late 1950s. We have newspaper reporter Andrew Genzoli to thank for that. In 1958, he wrote a tongue-in-cheek feature for the *Humboldt Times* in California about a crew of loggers working close to Bluff Creek. After a weekend away from the job site, the loggers came back to find sets of large footprints — three different sizes — around their machines.

In a personal column, Genzoli wrote, "Maybe we have a cousin of the Abominable Snowman of the Himalayas" here in Humboldt County. Surely, the story sold some papers. But — to history — the most important part of Genzoli's reporting came in what he called the creatures, what the loggers had called the creatures. Big Foot.

Ah, Bigfoot. In its complexity of description, the name is on par with walkie talkie or woodpecker. Obvious.

Now, "Sasquatch" sounds older, more believable, somehow. That's probably because its creator wasn't a newspaper man but a Canadian First Nations tribe in the Pacific Northwest. The coastal Salish people called the creature "Sasq'ets." The Hupa tribe of northern California call them Oh-mah-ah, or O-mah for short. But all the names really come down to "hairy men" or "wild men" of the woods.

Maybe the first wild man to ever be recorded was the hair-covered Enkidu in the ancient Sumerian Epic of Gilgamesh. Legends of the Woodwose, those wild, hair-covered men have been passed down for centuries in England.

One of the earliest recorded Bigfoot reports in North America goes back to 1811. Canadian trader named David Thompson said he discovered huge tracks in the Rockies near Jasper, Alberta. They were 14 inches long and 8 inches wide. Logger Albert Ostman said he was kidnapped in British Columbia by a Sasquatch family in 1924 and held for six days.

But the name Bigfoot did more to capture the American public's attention on the creature than the centuries of sightings and folklore ever did. Somethings big, hairy, and unknown were out in the woods. Now the boogeymen had a lovable name — a banner — that the public could all gather beneath. And, maybe more than anything, Genzoli's stories (and there were several) ignited a fire about Bigfoot in America.

It was thanks to those Bigfoot stories that Roger Patterson and Bob Gimlin went searching for the creature around Willow Creek. And they captured the still-undisputed, and best piece of Bigfoot evidence ever — The Patterson Gimlin Film. You know the film, even if you don't know its name. Brown and grainy with a dark human-like figure walking away and giving a heart-stopping look back at the camera in mid-stride.

And Bigfoot's flame hasn't dimmed here. If anything, Bigfoot is bigger than ever. But these creatures in America didn't start with Genzoli and Bluff Creek or even Willow Creek. Dig around newspaper archives for the terms "wild man" or "hairy man" in the United States, and you'll find a treasure trove of amazing stories (and they ain't cute like *Harry and the Hendersons*).

The stories are of a wild man — or a wood devil — terrorizing Union encampments during the Civil War. Or of a rash of sightings so terrifying that they sparked maybe the first organized Bigfoot hunt in America. Then there's that story of that famous pioneer who failed to heed that ominous warning from that strange creature in the woods of what would become Texas.

A man-beast in camp

It was a massive collection, a seeming mountain of autographs and old letters. They'd been lovingly collected, but it was time for them go. The appraisers arrived days before the estate sale and began their work. They combed through that mountain of old papers, sorting them and authenticating them the best they could.

This was 1999 in Hartford, Connecticut. But a found letter from Private James Moore of the Pennsylvania 67th Infantry Regiment, Company K soon transported the whole scene back to 1863 on a cold February night in Harper's Ferry, Virginia.

"...Ramsey and myself were charged to guard Company accoutrements along the railway. Very cold still night...

"...the boys started raising a ruckus from the garrison. Some were yelling aloud, that a man-beast was on foot. There was rifle fire towards the river. We continued our duty as the yelling and shots continued...

"...the Corporal queried the witnesses from the Company. I was told that the devil raided the food stores after climbing the wall...

"...it was covered in thick layers of dark hair...
"...maybe 8 foot from head to toe."

The beast of the Hiwassee

In a discovery similar to the letter of Private Moore, a man was helping his grandmother sort through her attic. There, they found the diary of his great-great-grandfather, MW Cooper. This is all from a fan writing to a YouTuber called Blue Ridge Bigfoot.

Bivouacked there on the bank of the Hiwassee River near Chattanooga, the other men in camp wanted to hear fiddle tunes. They begged Cooper to play them. But he was a gifted musician, classically trained on the violin — not the fiddle — at Oberlin College. Conscripted to fight in the Union army, Cooper insisted he take his beloved violin along with him.

In his leisure time, Cooper played. But he wanted to play Bach and Mozart. The other men in camp wanted to hear what Cooper called "garish folk music." The August sun "scorches my back and the air is so heavy and wet. The uniform that looks so grand in parades has become a burden for me too great to bare." Yet he did bare it. Bared it to play his beloved music on his own there on the bank of the Hiwassee.

Cooper tracked the river about a half mile away from camp. He sat down, watching the water slide by, and he began to play. It was the *Violin Sonata in G Minor* by Giuseppe Tartini, better know as the the Devil's Trill Sonata.

"As I was playing a large, dark shape appeared on the bank of the other side of the river, just visible through the brush," the man said in at the letter. "I stopped playing for a moment, thinking it was a bear. I questioned myself whether or not a bear could be that big.

"Shortly after the music stopped, the beast —whatever is was — retreated back into the woods. There was a river between us and it was a clear day. I began to play again.

"No sooner did I start than the creature reappeared. This time, I could see that it was not a bear and it walked on two legs like a man. Yet, this creature was far larger than any man. For some reason I was not afraid. The creature stood at the bank and made a movement in my direction.

"I did notice an unusual behavior as we locked eyes. The creature seemed to sway from side to side. I would have sworn it was listening to my sonata. When I finished the monster swiftly disappeared back into the wood."

That night, Cooper was awakened by a long and mournful howl that seemed to get longer and louder. The camp outside was eerily silent. He rolled to his side and could see that all the men around him were awake, too.

"One soldier whispered to us about the legend of a wild man that walked the Hiwassee River," the man said. "It was twice the size of any man, fearless and would give chase to anyone on foot or on horse. He described some gruesome scenes and suggested we not leave the tent."

No one did.

"I laid awake for hours thinking how close I could've been to my own death," he said. "How foolish had I become? My beautiful rendition of the Devil's Trill Sonata may have attracted a beast to our camp. As we broke camp the next day, no one mentioned the eerie howl but I know they heard it, too."

Private Moore was killed just a few weeks after that strange encounter on the banks of the Hiwassee. In a small skirmish with Confederates, he was shot in the chest.

The man mountain of the Okefenokee

Even before the Civil War, Southern pioneers recorded numerous sightings of "wild men." Traces of some of those encounters can still be found in newspapers from all over the country dating way back.

In 1829 the *Milledgeville Statesman*, a newspaper in Georgia, carried a story about a man and boy. They'd both heard Creek Nation tales of an enchanted island deep in the Okefenokee Swamp. There lived "mortals of super-human dimensions and incomparable beauty" as the Native Americans told it.

It'd been a dry spell that summer of 1829, and the man and the boy new they could push deep into the swamp and, perhaps, find that mysterious island. The progress of two weeks brought them to a "print of a foot-step so unearthly in its dimensions, so ominous of power, and terrible in form."

The print was 18 inches long and 9 inches across, the stride of this beast was over 6 feet. Their curiosity satisfied, the man and the boy made a hasty retreat out of the swamp. Back home, they quickly spread the tale of the "Man Mountain."

On the Florida side of the Okefenokee, hunters heard the tale and scoffed. They'd find this island and this Man Mountain. What they'd do when they found them, who knows? But they quickly set out into wet, dense heat of the Okefenokee. Within days, they were onto a set of tracks unlike anything they'd ever seen before.

They camped up on a ridge and things happened quickly. Two shots rang out as members of the party fired upon a "ferocious wild beast" charging at them. Wild in its terror and anger, the beast unleashed a scream that shook the swamp and most certainly laid fear into the hearts of those hunters.

The band of men gathered up closely, shouldering their rifles, leveling them right at the chest of the massive, hairy, heaving beast before them. But those rifles did not scare the animal. It lunged undaunted into the scrum of men. And for it, the beast was shot seven times. For a moment, they weren't sure the shots fazed the thing. In its vengeful wrath, the beast pulled down five men, wringing their heads off their bodies, as the story goes.

But it didn't last long. That wild, unbelievable monster began to slow, its arms getting heavier with each dangerous swing. Its piercing howl softened to a low growl. It hit the ground with a thud and wallowed, gave one last long roar, rolled, and finally stopped breathing.

The four surviving hunters edged in toward the body for a closer look. Their hearts were still pounding, but they'd risked a whole lot and had traveled a long way. An unquenchable fascination to see this thing was on them. But then fear was quickly back on the men. What if this beast wasn't the only one? What if its friends or family heard the commotion and were on the way?

They gathered their gear and headed quickly out of the Okefenokee Swamp. Back home, they said the wild, hairy beast was 13 feet tall.

The Arkansas Wild Man

Crowley's Ridge is a topographical oddity. It rises 250 feet to 500 feet above the pancake-flat plain of the Arkansas delta. Just west of Memphis, it stretches 150 miles from Helena, Arkansas, all the way north across the Missouri boot heel. It's a bit like The Wall in *Game of Thrones* but, y'know, natural, and in Arkansas.

Crowley's Ridge was no doubt wild and unsettled in the 1830s and 1840s. That's about the time the strangeness began. That strangeness would turn to fear. That fear would turn to desperation, anger and, finally, into action.

"His track measures 22 inches, his toes are as long as a common man's fingers," reported the *Baltimore Sun* in March 1846, "and in height and make, he is double the usual size."

Reports of a "wild man" in the area preceded that newspaper story by some years, some as early as 1834. Reports were focused around St. Francis, Greene, and Poinsett Counties, just a stone's throw from Memphis, right across the Mississippi River. It's unclear what was seen or what happened in the area after that story ran in the *Baltimore Sun*. But something clearly was seen and something clearly did happen.

Because by 1851, *The Patriot and State Gazette* of New Hampshire newspaper said an expedition was forming to find this "wild man." And a posse led by well-respected men of the community reportedly left Memphis on horseback that year in what might have been the first organized Bigfoot hunt in American history.

The Arkansas wild man was "of gigantic size and covered with hair," and it had been seen by hunters and farmers. Once the Wild Man had been seen chasing a herd of cattle, running away from two men, and leaping some 12 feet to 14 feet at a time.

Four years later, the *Pittsfield Sun* reported "a wild man, seven feet high, is stated to be roaming through the great Mississippi bottom in Arkansas. Numerous travelers and hunters have asserted that they have seen him, but none have been able to get near enough to give particulars concerning the strange being." That same year, the *Wisconsin Patriot* said the Wild Man was seen breaking the ice of a frozen lake. He was "covered with hair of a brownish cast" and "well muscled."

After that, another expedition left this time from Louisiana to try and capture the beast and prove his existence. One man, according to newspaper reports, rode ahead of the posse, hoping to take the creature (and maybe the glory) on his own.

"The wild man saw the horse and rider, and he rushed frantically toward them, and in an instant dragged the hunter to the ground and tore him in a most dreadful manner, scratching out one of his eyes and injuring the other so much that his friends despaired over of the recovery of his sight, and it bit large pieces out of his shoulder and various parts of his body.

"The hunter's friends and a party of Choctaw hunters set off in pursuit of the creature. They chased it up into the Ouachita Mountains, which were then covered in snow from an unusually brutal winter. Conditions slowed down the hunters and the Wild Man slipped away from them."

Crockett and the beast

This all brings us back to that legendary pioneer hacking his way through the untamed wilds of Texas. If anybody ever called him Davy, it's hard to know. At least one historian said that if they did call him that, David Crockett didn't like it.

I've always believed David Crockett was a pioneer and statesman from Tennessee. Davy Crockett was a Disney character. Davy Crockett — King of the Wild Frontier — wrestled bears and rode alligators. David Crockett opposed Andrew Jackson's Indian Removal Act as a U.S. Congressman from Tennessee.

On that day he was hacking through Texas scrub land, Crockett was fresh off an 1835 campaign to re-claim his seat in the U.S. House of Representatives. He lost, losing to a one-legged man Huntsman (the description will make more sense later).

And after that stinging defeat, Crockett decided he'd leave behind his family in Tennessee, and take up with some fellows headed for new fortunes in Texas, or what was then the Mexican state of Tejas. Before he left, though, he famously told his constituents to kiss his...foot.

"Since you have chosen to elect a man with a timber toe to succeed me, you may all go to hell and I will go to Texas," Crockett said at a party in Memphis.

If he ever did regret burning that bridge, it didn't show. He'd been talking up Texas independence, even during the election. If Jackson's successor Martin Van Buren was elected, Crockett said he would head south and join the fight. He did. In January 1836, Crockett arrived in Nacogdoches, Texas, and signed an oath as a volunteer to the Provisional Government of Texas. Each volunteer was promised around 4,600 acres of land as payment.

After that, the men were hacking their way toward San Antonio in that dreadful Texas heat. Crockett looked at the sun high in the sky and decided it was a good time for a break. He told the rest to his brother-in law, Abner Burgin, in a letter.

"William and I were pushing through some thicket, clearing the way, when I sat down to mop my brow. I sat for a spell, watching as William made his good and fine progress. I removed my boots and sat with my rations, thinking the afternoon a fine time to lunch. As the birds whistled and chirped, and I ate my small and meager ration, I tapped my axe upon the opposite end of the felled tree I rested upon.

"Whether it was the axe's disturbance or possibly the heat of the sun which caused an apparition to slowly form in front of my eyes, I know not. As a Christian man, I swear to you, Abe, that what spirit came upon me was the shape and shade of a large ape man, the likes we might expect among the more bellicose and hostile Indian tribes in the Territories.

"The shade formed into the most deformed and ugly countenance. Covered in wild hair, with small and needling eyes, large broken rows of teeth, and the height of three foundlings, I spit upon the ground the bread I was eating.

"The monster then addressed a warning to me. Abner, it told me to return from Texas, to flee this fort and to abandon this lost cause. When I began to question this, the creature spread upon the wind like the morning steam swirls off a frog pond. I swear to you, Abner, that whatever meat or sausage disagreed with me that afternoon, I swore off all beef and hog for a day or so afterward."

Less than six months after he wrote that letter, Crockett gave his life defending The Alamo.

13

Little Green Men of Kentucky

A plea for help

The dark highway was deserted and mercifully peaceful. But his hands still shook on the wheel. The only other car on the road was behind him. He checked for their lights in his rearview mirror so often he was driving himself crazy. But he had to know they were still back there, still OK.

In his glances back, he'd scan the back seat at the stunned faces his family, especially the little ones. They stared vacantly out of the window or straight ahead at that lonesome stretch of highway, lit only by the beams of the headlights.

He knew their minds weren't on the way to Hopkinsville, like the truck was. Their minds were back at the house, back in Kelly. Back with what had been the most surreal and violent night of their lives.

His mind was there, too, if he was being honest. He could keep the truck in the road, but his thoughts were all over the place. They ran from this scene to that one, from the unbelievable story that started the night to the gunfire that finally ended it. Or so he thought.

Maybe his ears still rang from the gun battle. Maybe the smell of gunpowder was still in his nose. It was late and he hadn't had any sleep. But none would come soon, he thought. Adrenaline coursed through his veins. All of it together and any thought he had about what he'd seen that night got his hands shaking on that steering wheel.

But he had to be tough, just for a little while longer, he thought. The police station was just a few miles away. There, he'd get help, help protecting his family and help, maybe, to sort out just what had happened that hot August night.

But would the police believe him, he wondered? Surely, with so many of us and with such a long experience, but...still he just wasn't sure. A big gun battle like that has got to leave some sort of evidence, right? Blood or something, surely. Right?

He almost didn't care, as he rolled into the police station parking lot. Whatever those things were...he just wanted it over. He wanted the police to tell him that his family was safe. But as he built that wall of confidence around him, the visions of those...things...approaching the house tore that wall back down brick by brick, exposing his soft, naked fear. A fear of the unknown, and an unknown threat.

That night in 1955, the man and his family were attacked, attacked by beings that seemed immune to bullets. These beings — about a dozen of them — were small, gray and silvery in the light, with massive black eyes, and pointed ears. Aliens, it seemed, had invaded Kelly, Kentucky.

Myths and misconceptions

Did you know you can't see the Great Wall of China from space? That's according to NASA. Not me.

Salt doesn't make water boil any faster. Napoleon wasn't short. You can swim right after you eat. Bats aren't blind. And you don't have to wait 24 hours to file a missing persons report.

Call them myths or misconceptions, somehow these ideas spring to the top of the collective zeitgeist and slouch around up there like a stubborn, old mule.

Anyone reading this book (and just about anyone else, I'd wager) knows about "little green men." They're short, skinny, with big heads, and large eyes, and they run around naked — all that bright green skin out there for anyone to see.

But, according to some of the characters in today's story, they never called them "little green men." They said "little gray men," maybe, but never, ever green. But from this event, the world forever got the phrase "little green men" — and it came from Kentucky.

The color hardly mattered to the folks in the story. They survived a night under attack from a foe that was unrelenting and unknown in identity and intention. Maybe worse, those folks would survive years — decades — of harsh scrutiny and ridicule for stepping forward about what happened to them that crazy, hot August night.

A family get-together

Kelly is in western Kentucky, just about eight miles north of Hopkinsville, which is about 80 miles northwest of Nashville. Back in Kelly, drive out Old Madisonville Road and you'll find the old Gaither McGehee farm. Back in 1955, the farmhouse belonged to Elmer "Lucky" Sutton. On August 21st, the house was hopping with all the doin's for a Sunday-night, family dinner.

Sutton's mother Glennie Lankford filled the house with her children Lonnie, Charlton, and Mary. There were two sons from a previous marriage, Lucky and John Charley, or "J.C." There were their wives, Vera and Alene, Alene's brother, O.P. Baker. Billy Ray Taylor and his wife, June, were there visiting from Pennsylvania. Then you add all their kids, and that little farmhouse was packed.

At about 7 p.m., Billy Ray stepped out of the back of the house to get a bucket of water from the well. As he lowered the bucket, Billy Ray said he saw a light and then what he said looked like a flying saucer land in a field about a city block away behind the house. There was no explosion, only a kind of hissing sound. Totally perplexed and probably a little scared, Billy Ray went back in the house with that bucket of water.

He was excited and began telling everyone there that he'd seen a spaceship land right behind the house. They dismissed him right off the bat. It was a falling star, they said. But they didn't dismiss him for very long. Within an hour, Lucky's dog started barking violently. The men ran outside just in time to see the animal turn tail and hide under the house.

Attack of the Little Men

Here's how *Kentucky New Era* columnist Annie McFie described the entire first volley of the Kelly alien invasion.

"Approaching from the fields was a luminous shape — a humanoid figure three and a half feet tall, shining all over as if 'nickel-plated.' Large, pointed ears extended from its oversized head, and its eyes, set more laterally than human eyes, glowed with yellow light. Its thin arms reached almost to the ground, displaying big, webbed hands with talons at the ends of the fingers.

"Apparently, the creature had seen its share of cowboy movies — it raised its hands high over its head in an attitude of surrender. Ignoring Mrs. Lankford's pleas not to shoot at it, her son and Taylor opened fire on the intruder with a shotgun and a .22. To their astonishment, it flipped over, righted itself, and ran off into the darkness.

"Presently, it — or a second one like it — appeared looking in a window. Lucky's younger brother J.C. discharged the shotgun through the window-screen, knocking the being out of sight.

"Certain it had been hit, Billy Ray, followed by Lucky, started outside to find it. As Billy Ray hesitated beneath an overhanging roof, those in the house began to scream at the sight of a claw-like hand reaching down to touch his hair.

"Billy Ray was quickly pulled back inside, and Lucky leapt out into the yard, and blasted the creature off the roof with the shotgun.

"Billy Ray spotted another being, and both men shot it out of the maple tree in which it was perched. It floated, rather than fell to the ground and scurried away on slender, inflexible legs that seemed to move from the hip only.

"Just then, another entity (possibly the one that had been on the roof) appeared around the corner of the house right near Lucky. His shotgun pellets struck it point-blank with a sound like that of a metal bucket. Nonetheless, it jumped up and ran away unhurt.

"Several more times the aliens advanced on the house, never making any sound nor behaving with any overt hostility and each time they were repelled by a hail of gunfire.

"At last, the unnerved defenders fled from the farmhouse in two cars and raced for the Hopkinsville police station where, in a state of near-hysteria, they told their bizarre story."

A police investigation

Hopkinsville Police Chief Russell Greenwell thought they were joking. But if they were, man, what a joke. Eleven people — and little kids — all acting like they were scared out of their minds and telling the same insane story all to pull a prank on one of the highest-ranking law enforcement officials in Christian County. Now that is quite a joke.

But finally, they persuaded the police to follow them back to Lucky's house. It must've been eerie pulling back into that darkened driveway that they'd left in such a panic not long before. But I bet they all felt a lot better about it with all those police cars behind them.

Chief Greenwell brought about 20 officers to the scene. And they'd called the feds, too. They sent Army reservist Major John Albert to Kelly that night. At the time, he just happened to be at Camp Campbell (what's now called Fort Campbell in nearby Clarksville, Tennessee).

All of them had a look around the yard, the fields around house, and all through the house. They found four boxes of spent .22 shells and an untold number of shotgun shells. They found that hole in the window screen where J.C. had shot at one of the little men.

Out back, they found a luminous patch of grass under a fence. Lucky told them that's where one of the little men had been shot. No one could explain it. And no one ever will because no one took a sample.

Then a loud, long squall from nowhere made everybody jump and had the officers grabbing for their pistols. They looked all around the dark scene with their hearts pounding. When the officer closest to the sound looked down, he realized he'd stepped on a cat's tail.

Chief Greenwell said that he and the other investigators admitted to each other that a "weird feeling" permeated the entire area that night. Although he couldn't find any evidence of what, exactly, happened, "Something scared those people," he said. "Something beyond reason, nothing ordinary."

Officers were reluctant to express opinion on what they'd seen or in the story of the little men. But they agreed on one thing. Nobody at Lucky's house had been drinking that night.

With the excitement over and nothing more to do, everyone but those occupying the farmhouse left at around 2 a.m. Maybe those little, silvery, metallic men watched them leave from somewhere dark and just out of sight. Because just as soon as all of those police officers left, the little men came back, peeking through a window.

Lucky shouldered his shotgun and fired, blasting yet another hole in a window screen. But, again, the shot had no effect on the creature at all. There'd be no rest for the 11 people staying at the Sutton house that night. The little, silvery men — for that is how all of the witnesses described them to police — came calling back at the house until dawn broke.

That next morning, the little men were gone but the police came back. They had a longer and better look around the farm in the daylight. But they didn't find anything. The rest of the world, however, found Lucky Sutton's farmhouse way out on Old Madisonville Road in Kelly, Kentucky.

The story gets out

Paducah Sun-Democrat August 25, 1955

HOPKINSVILLE, KY. — "Those green-eyed little men from outer space may have been bright-eyed monkeys from a circus passing through. That, at least, is the theory advanced by an unidentified male resident of Hopkinsville.

The man suggested that a circus truck loaded with monkeys stopped for some time in the area Sunday night. The man also indicated that the circus keeper may have let some of the monkeys out for exercise.

At any rate, local officers have been the brunt of much heckling since the widespread publicity regarding the 12 to 15 little green men.

Said Deputy Sheriff George Batts of Christian County: "Everywhere you turn somebody is asking you about the little men. Whether you're on foot or driving along in the patrol car, somebody finds an opportunity to say, 'Say, have you seen any little men today?'"

Did you catch it? Right there in that tiny story buried back on page 21, the creatures magically morph from little green-eyed men to little green men. Notice that Deputy Batts didn't say that in his quote. He said "little men," and he said it twice.

Little green men. How? Why? No one is really sure. But here's how Wikipedia explains it: "Employing journalistic license and deviating from the witnesses' accounts, many newspaper articles used the term 'little green men' in writing up the story."

But the *Sun-Democrat* reporter wasn't the only one to use little green men to describe the Kelly creatures. Hordes of reporters from all over the country descended on Old Madisonville Road to glimpse the Sutton farmhouse and, maybe, a little man of their own.

Among them were a reporter and photographer from Hopkinsville's *Kentucky New Era*. When they got there, someone had hung a sign in a tree. Where the "no trespassing" sign used to be, another sign now said "50 cent admission for spectators."

Only Glennie Lankford and her 7-year-old granddaughter remained in the house that morning. While she wasn't happy to have yet another reporter knock on her door, Glennie was at least glad that these were local.

"These people are worrying us to death," she told them. "Please tell them not to come here and worry us."

So many people came to see the spot, according to the newspaper, that the family had police there to keep the traffic moving. At around midnight, people were still coming. The parade began again the next morning.

"Mrs. Lankford and her family were reaping the the ill effects of fame," the *New Era* story said. "Stories of about how the family had battled the 12 to 15 little men who apparently got off the space ship have appeared in almost every newspaper in the United States. Leading news commentators in TV and radio have made numerous references to the little men."

Still, Lankford remained steadfast.

"I only know what I saw," she told the *New Era* reporter. "I saw two of them. Or, maybe I saw the same one twice. I saw one about 10:30 p.m. and the other around 3:30 a.m. The second time, I watched this little man for more than a minute. I had gone to bed and was seeing him through the window."

The story remains

Anyone there that hot August night would have to talk about little green men the rest of their lives. Their decedents are still talking about them today. Geraldine Sutton Stith was only 7 or 8 years old when her father, Lucky, told her the story of what is now known as the Kelly-Hopkinsville Encounter.

By then, even Lucky was calling them green (because that how the story went). But he told his daughter they were actually silver. He told her they were about three feet tall, the size of a five-year-old. Their arms were double the length of humans' and they had pointed ears. He said the eyes were in the same place as humans, but were more of an almond shape. The eyes had a luminous glow. He said they really didn't walk, just skimmed on top of ground, but moved their legs.

Stith also explained why Lucky and Billy Ray shot at the creatures.

"He's just one of the kind of guys to see something like that and naturally think 'they're going to do something. I've got to protect my family.' I guess that's what he done. He bared arms and started laying into them. I'd have done the same thing. I'd have been aiming right between the eyes," she said.

Stith has written two books on the encounter: *Alien Legacy* and *The Kelly Green Men*. And when any of the creepy television shows want to talk about the Kelly-Hopkinsville Encounter, they go knocking on her door.

One thing that has bothered Stith all these years is the way that her family was characterized in the press, as a bunch of gun-toting hillbillies. Many reports also called them a "low-status group of people." Lucky and Billy Ray worked in the carnival, and reporters used that fact to discredit them. Papers tried to say that being in that line of work, somehow, made it easier for them to make up a story like that.

"They couldn't have made up something like that," Geraldine Stith said. "They were just country folks. They wouldn't have thought to think up something like that so elaborate. They wouldn't have run to town terrified in the middle of the night."

From Blue Book to Spielberg

The Kelly-Hopkinsville Encounter is one of the most famous and unique alien encounter stories in American history. While military officials said they didn't find any evidence of a UFO landing or of any little men around the farm, they sure studied the heck out of the Kelly case.

Dr. J. Allen Hyneck, head of the Air Force's Project Blue Book UFO investigation, went to Kelly, saw it for himself, and talked to eyewitnesses. He didn't find anything conclusive. But the Kelly chapter in the Blue Book report is one of the longest.

The Kelly encounter had a higher-profile fan than even Dr. Hyneck. Steven Spielberg was hot to follow up his blockbuster *Close Encounters of the Third Kind* with a blockbuster sequel. That film was to be called *Night Skies* and be based directly on the Kelly encounter.

It was going be scary. Eleven aliens were going to descend on a Kentucky farm and terrorize the locals. But Spielberg decided he wanted to go softer, sweeter. So, instead of *Night Skies*, the world got *E.T. the Extra Terrestrial*.

More than six decades after that frightful August night in Kelly, the town still celebrates it. Since 2011, proud Kelly residents have organized the Little Green Men Festival. It's celebrated every year right around the same time Lucky and Billy Ray were firing their guns at those little men that made the town famous.

At the beginning of the festival they had a kids alien costume contest, an "intergalactic trade show" with "out of this world" items. The Owensboro Symphony Orchestra played an evening of "out of this world music." There was an "out of this world" karaoke contest. I'll stop there.

No, I won't. The headline for the *Kentucky New Era* story about the festival in 2019 promised it would be (you guessed it) "out of this world." That year's festival had a county-fair vibe with rides, food, and a UFO bouncy house for kids.

There was also a 38-foot-wide flying saucer right in the middle of it all. Geraldine Stith, once again, told the encounter story the way she heard it from her dad, Lucky. But maybe the sweetest event of it all was the Glennie Lankford Outdoor Gospel Sing.

14

New Orleans, Of Course

On the trolley
New Orleans is unlike any other town in America. When I was down there in late 2019, reminders of its singularity were constant.

I was on the St. Charles street car line, sitting in the back of what most of America would call a trolley but in New Orleans is a street car. The cars run on grassy strips of land in the median of two traffic lanes. For seem reason, New Orleanians calls this strip the neutral ground. Oh, and those people on the side of the road? In New Orleans they're not walking on sidewalks but banquettes.

This street cars are tall, wide, with simple, curved lines plucked right out of the past. But they fit so perfectly into the context of modern New Orleans. The street cars are old, but they (mostly) run on time. It's a blend of tradition and utility. Much like so many aspects of New Orleans culture. Old things — music, recipes, architecture — still work and are adapted to modern times. Think of the way brass bands are embracing hip-hop.

Blend it all together, and New Orleanians call, simply, the culture, and the city takes that culture seriously. It's literally everywhere you look. For example, the trees along St. Charles are usually draped in Mardi Gras beads. Even that remnant from Mardi Gras parades is celebrated in pictures, and film, and there's even a restaurant on St.

Charles called The Beaded Oak. This celebration of New Orleans singularity doesn't seem precious to me, over the top cutesy. It just seems completely baked in to everyday life.

So, if the city has its own language, own music, own food, and everything else, it's little surprise that they have their own distinct paranormal traditions, too. Instead of just a werewolf, they have the rougarou. The Bigfoot down there is the Honey Island Swamp Monster. An 18th century serial killer — one who called himself a demon and a devil — showed his pride in New Orleans culture in a very specific, terrifying way.

No discussion of New Orleans and the paranormal would be complete without talking about ghosts, of course. Some have called New Orleans the most haunted city in America. I guess New Orleans and Savannah can fight it out over that title.

While you might not want to buy a haunted house, it seems everyone wants to visit a haunted city. A dozen or so New Orleans tour companies each offer three of four different haunted tours every day. Now, if you're trying to sell your house, you may not advertise that your house is haunted. But New Orleans official wills talk about the city's ghosts to anyone who will listen. There's even a haunted itinerary page on the city's tourism website.

Jean Lafitte's Blacksmith Shop Bar

Bourbon Street ain't for everyone. It's loud, crowded, littered, and kind of smelly. But it's a one-of-kind Southern and American experience you should try at least once. If for nothing else, head to a quieter section of Bourbon and look for the ghost of a famous pirate.

Built somewhere between 1722 and 1732, Lafitte's Blacksmith Shop stands on the corner of Bourbon Street and St. Phillip. It is the oldest structure in America to ever be used as a bar, but don't let that fool you.

Inside, it's lively with laughter, conversation, frozen daiquiri machines, sports on television, and everything else you'd expect at an American bar. But the old, brick building is dark inside, too. Shadows lurk on the exposed wooden beams of the low ceilings. Over by the fireplace on the first floor, it smells flinty, smokey, and can almost transport you back to that time in history.

The bar is named for famed pirate Jean Lafitte. The pirate is also famous for aiding General Andrew Jackson during the Battle of New Orleans in 1814. As the British lay at the mouth of the Mississippi River, Lafitte rushed powder, flint, and troops to Jackson at Chalmette. The troops and supplies helped Jackson win that decisive victory, effectively ending the War of 1812.

Sometime between 1772 and 1791, the property is believed to have been used by Jean and and his brother, Pierre, as a New Orleans base for their Barataria smuggling operation. But, as the bar says on its website, "Like most New Orleans legends, Lafitte's Blacksmith Shop is a gumbo of truth and French, Spanish, African, Cajun, and American embellishments." If you can't count on the story, though, count on Jean Lafitte's ghost.

Sightings of the pirate's ghost are so frequent, they're almost commonplace. According to New-Orleans-based Ghost City Tours, Lafitte is seen as a full-bodied apparition, usually over by that flinty, smokey fireplace on the first floor. The tour company says the spirit never speaks to anyone or interacts with them at all. He simply appears and stares until he's noticed.

Another ghost, a woman, is seen on the bar's second floor. Another ghost there whispers your name in your ear. Glasses, bottles, and silverware have reportedly flown off the bar unexpectedly. Also, piercing red eyes have been seen in the bar's dark corners. They stare until you stare back and then they fade away.

The many ghosts of New Orleans

But, if you can't find Jean Lafitte at his blacksmith's shop, walk — maybe on the same route as Lafitte — over to the Old Absinthe

House. The 200-year-old bar was where Lafitte would meet with General Jackson to discuss terms and plans for the Battle of New Orleans. Guests and employees said they've seen the ghosts of both at the bar. Doors open and close on their own and bottles and glasses move there, too.

Walk across the Quarter to Arnaud's, the high society restaurant, and you might catch a glimpse of a young girl in a Mardi Gras gown. She's said to be the long-dead daughter of restaurant founder, Arnaud Cazenave.

A Storyville madame haunts the Bombay Club. An insane and maybe murderous pharmacist haunts the Pharmacy Museum. Investigators have recorded electromagnetic activity, temperature changes, electronic voice phenomena, and more at an 1872 mansion called The Haunted Mortuary. Look to the second story of Napoleon House at night and you may just catch the shade of a Civil War soldier dressed in gray.

St. Louis Cemetery No. 1 is a little creepy, even if it ain't haunted. There you'll find the above-ground crypt of famed voodoo priestess Marie Laveau and the future tomb of actor Nicolas Cage.

William Faulkner is said to still inhabit the French Quarter house where he wrote his first book. Employees of what is now called Faulkner House Books say they've seen the figure of the man and sometimes smell his burning pipe.

An 1834 house fire led to the discovery of enslaved people chained up in Madame Lalurie's torture chamber in her French Quarter mansion. Current owners say they'll sometimes see body imprints on beds no one has slept on, doors swinging shut, and faucets turning on by themselves.

Tennessee Williams wrote *The Rose Tattoo* at the Hotel Monteleone. Numerous guests and employees say he's still there. Other ghosts, those of former employees and children, are seen regularly on the hotel's hallways. Up on the 14th, floor look for Maurice, the spirit of a young boy who lost his parents and is said to search the hotel for them to this day.

Honey Island Swamp Monster

Harlan Ford and Billy Mills came out of the Honey Island Swamp in 1974 with large tracks they casted while out on hunting trip. The tracks weren't that big, but they were four-toed from a webbed foot.

A decade before they produced those tracks, the two hunters said they'd encountered a large creature in the swamp. It was about 7 feet tall they said, with grayish hair all over its body. It stared at them with large, amber eyes. But the creature got away, they said, and rain washed away its footprints.

Ford passed away in 1980, and it's said that his widow discovered a reel of Super 8 among his things. On that jumpy, grainy tape was a hulking, dark figure standing on two legs at maybe 7 feet tall. The figure moves in and out of a tree line, leaving it mostly obscured.

Researchers got the film and studied it. They found the production suspicious. First off, you couldn't see much of the thing in the film. Also, the beginning and the end of the film was missing. The researcher was inconclusive. They couldn't tell if the whole thing was a hoax.

Searching for answers, researchers headed back to Louisiana, back to the Honey Island Swamp. Many who lived around there, though, told them they'd never seen any monster and never really believed the hunters' tale. Then, in 2011, a pair of shoes were discovered buried in the mud around a hunting camp. The shoes were four toed with webbed feet.

But Dana Holyfield believes. She's Ford's granddaughter and she made a documentary called *The Legend of the Honey Island Swamp Monster*. She's also been featured on shows like *Mysteries at the Museum*, *Fact of Faked*, *Swamp People*, and more.

Many of the tales I've heard about the Honey Island Swamp

Monster ain't about Ford's four-toed, made-up monster. And it ain't some humanoid/alligator hybrid. The creature I've heard described is more like the one described in Dana Holyfield's documentary.

The Honey Island Swamp Monster I know (and love) is basically a Bigfoot living in the swamp, much like Arkansas' Fouke Monster. It's tall, covered in dark hair, and comes complete with that trademark odor guaranteed to make a skunk gag.

Holyfield's film features men who have had encounters with the creature. I don't think they're acting. I don't think they're making it up. They're the Cajun versions of the good ole boys I grew up with. So, while a tall tale comes easy with a beer in your hand, everything changes when a video camera comes on.

"I thought it was a dog, one man says, and then it stood up."

"Then I turned on my little flashlight on them and seen them footprints and I through, oh, shoot, them ain't human," another man said. But he didn't say shoot.

"That thing was big enough to come into this camp and tear everything up," says another.

"I didn't know if it was man or beast," a man says. "I'd never seen anything like that before."

The Honey Island Swamp is about an hour north of New Orleans, close to the Mississippi border. It's close enough that about half a dozen companies run tourists from the French Quarter to the swamp every day. But Honey Island couldn't be more different than Bourbon Street.

There, the knees of bald cypress trees gnarl up out of the muddy water. Spanish moss drips from those cypress and wild tupelo trees, hanging and swaying like massive ghosts over the water. Wild boar and alligators swim right up to tour boats looking for a bite to eat. At times duckweed lays on top of the water spreading among the trees and undergrowth like an unbelievable green carpet.

By day, it's easy to admit to yourself that something wild and beyond our knowledge could live and thrive in such a dense, unknowable place. By night, that idle curiosity about such things amps up to full-blown nightmare fuel.

No matter what evidence has ever been found or any hoax that's been discovered of the legend of the Honey Island Swamp Monster, the story will remain the same. The monster is a humanoid figure 7 feet tall. It'll have the massive and hair covered body of a man, feet like an alligator, and strange yellow eyes.

Listen to such a tale long enough, and you might get the monster's origin story. You see, a circus train was heading to New Orleans, but it crashed. When it did, an ape escaped into the swamp. There, it mated with an alligator and — *tada!* — Honey Island Swamp Monster.

The Axeman

He loved jazz, apparently. It was maybe something he'd fallen in love with in New Orleans. Maybe he took it back home with him to Tartarus, wherever that is. No one has ever known. But he didn't come to New Orleans to tool around Jackson Square or eat a bowl of gumbo. He came to kill. And that's just what he did for two years.

He'd sneak into the city — usually into grocery store owned by Italians — and find his prey. He'd go around to the back door and use a chisel to remove a panel. He'd slip inside and leave the panel and chisel on the floor. He'd prowl around the house until he found a straight razor or, preferably, an axe. That's how he got his name — the Axeman.

The killing spree began mysteriously in May 1918. The killer eluded police with the only piece of evidence, really, being that the killer targeted Italian families. The attacks were clearly racially motivated. But while some claimed them to be the work of the mafia, police believed they were in fact just the work of a "fiend." That's how New Orleans Police superintendent Frank Mooney put it. He said the Axeman had "a Jekyll and Hyde personality, like Jack the

Ripper. ... [S]uddenly the impulse to kill comes upon him and he must obey it."

The Axeman continued his bloody work, even crossing over the Mississippi River to Gretna, where he badly injured a man named Charlie Cortimiglia and his wife, Rose, and killed their two-year-old daughter.

After this, the Axeman seemed to vanish. But not before penning a famous note to the city that is so wild, that I'm just going to let you read the whole thing right here:

"Hell, March 13, 1919

Esteemed Mortals of New Orleans:

The Axeman

They have never caught me and they never will. They have never seen me, for I am invisible, even as the ether that surrounds your earth. I am not a human being, but a spirit and a demon from the hottest hell. I am what you Orleanians and your foolish police call the Axeman.

When I see fit, I shall come and claim other victims. I alone know whom they shall be. I shall leave no clue except my bloody axe, besmeared with blood and brains of he whom I have sent below to keep me company.

If you wish you may tell the police to be careful not to rile me. Of course, I am a reasonable spirit. I take no offense at the way they have conducted their investigations in the past. In fact, they have been so utterly stupid as to not only amuse me, but His Satanic Majesty, Francis Josef, etc. But tell them to beware. Let them not try to discover what I am, for it were better that they were never born than to incur the wrath of the Axeman. I don't think there is any need of such a warning, for I feel sure the police will always dodge me, as they have in the past. They are wise and know how to keep away from all harm.

Undoubtedly, you Orleanians think of me as a most horrible

murderer, which I am, but I could be much worse if I wanted to. If I wished, I could pay a visit to your city every night. At will I could slay thousands of your best citizens (and the worst), for I am in close relationship with the Angel of Death.

Now, to be exact, at 12:15 (earthly time) on next Tuesday night, I am going to pass over New Orleans. In my infinite mercy, I am going to make a little proposition to you people. Here it is:

I am very fond of jazz music, and I swear by all the devils in the nether regions that every person shall be spared in whose home a jazz band is in full swing at the time I have just mentioned. If everyone has a jazz band going, well, then, so much the better for you people. One thing is certain and that is that some of your people who do not jazz it out on that specific Tuesday night (if there be any) will get the axe.

Well, as I am cold and crave the warmth of my native Tartarus, and it is about time I leave your earthly home, I will cease my discourse. Hoping that thou wilt publish this, that it may go well with thee, I have been, am, and will be the worst spirit that ever existed either in fact or realm of fancy.

--The Axeman"

New Orleans perfectly pulsed with jazz that night, as the story goes. The Axeman took not one more soul.

Beware the Rougarou

When the French came to Louisiana, they brought their culture with them. Much of that still lingers in the food, language, architecture, and more. The French also brought a werewolf with them.

They called him the loup garou — or wolf man. The loup garou was a terror on the edges of French towns and villages for centuries. Unexplained deaths of people and animals were blamed on the loup garou. In fact, the beast was the scapegoat for much of whatever French villagers couldn't explain.

So, when those boats docked in New Orleans, the loup garou got right off with the brand-new Americans. Later, the beast became a bit more American, too. By the time America had turned those French and French Canadians into Cajuns, the loup garou became the Rougarou.

In the Cajun legends, the creature is said to prowl the swamps around Acadiana and Greater New Orleans, and the sugar cane fields and woodlands of the regions. The Rougarou most often is described as a creature with a human body and the head of a wolf or dog. Tales of the Rougarou have inspired fear and, maybe, obedience into an untold number of Cajun children. Also, the Rougarou is said to hunt down and kill Catholics who don't follow the rules of Lent for seven years in a row.

One legend says the Rougarou is a person under a spell for 101 days. After that, the spell is broken when he bites and draws blood from another human. That person is then cursed to become a rougarou.

If you want to see the Rougarou, head to New Orleans. The creature — or a mock-up of the creature — is on display at the Audubon Zoo. The Rougarou stands at least 7 feet tall with sharp claws at the end of long fingers stretched out to nab its next victim. Wild eyes splay over a snout filled with razor-sharp teeth. Real or not, the Rougarou at the zoo is terrifying, even more so at night when they bathe the entire exhibit in a blood-red light.

The Rougarou legend is strong in southern Louisiana. Consider that back when the New Orleans Hornets (now Pelicans) were looking for a new team name, they trademarked the name The Rougarous.

15

Haint Blue

What is haint blue?

Haint blues are colors. Well, haint blue is really just many shades of light blue. I've made it complicated.

But one thing is simple. The most traditional purpose of painting a part of your house haint blue is to keep away ghosts or evil spirits. Throughout the South for centuries, the most traditional place people paint their house haint blue is the ceiling of the front porch.

Haint blue originated with the Gullah Geechee people, descendants of African slaves brought to the Sea Islands of South Carolina, North Carolina, Georgia, and Florida. If you've never heard of haint blue before, you certainly do know some of the cultural gifts the Gullah-Geechee have bestowed upon American society.

Let's load up and head out to the Sea Islands. Let's open our ears to the beautiful music that is the Gullah-Geechee language. Let's also explore a rich culture that — germane to this book — includes folk magic, hoodoo, conjure doctors, and, of course, haint blue.

Heartbreaking silence

In the end, the young man made a heartbreaking decision. It was one that followed him, even marked him for the rest of his life and, eventually — for good or bad — became his trademark.

The young man grew up in Pin Point, Georgia, a poor, rural

African-American community near Savannah. And when he spoke, people could quickly pinpoint his Pin Point roots, and you know how kids can be.

The young man grew up speaking Gullah, sometimes called Geechee in Georgia. It was long thought of as a pidgin English that, back then, made the speaker sound uneducated to the well-to-do. That's the way the little boy felt, I'm sure.

Gullah or Geechee was the language the little boy spoke at home. But not when he went to school. In fact, he finally and heartbreakingly decided to kind of stop talking at school altogether.

So many years after his decision, here's what that young man (grown to be an adult by then) told the *New York Times* about it, "When I was 16, I was sitting as the only black kid in my class, and I had grown up speaking a kind of a dialect ... called Geechee. Some people call it Gullah, and people praise it now. But they used to make fun of us back then. It's not standard English.

"So I learned that, and I just started developing the habit of listening. And it just got to be, I didn't ask questions in college or law school.

"For all those reasons and a few others, I just think that it's more in my nature to listen rather than to ask a bunch of questions. The only reason I could see for asking the questions is to let people know I've got something to ask. That's not a legitimate reason in the Supreme Court of the United States."

That quiet little boy grew up to be the famously quiet U.S. Supreme Court Justice Clarence Thomas.

Meet the Gullah Geechee

Estimates put the number of Gullah Geechee people from 250,000 to nearly a million. They are all the direct descendants of West African slaves brought to the U.S. in the 1700s. Most of those slaves were brought specifically to the Sea Islands because they knew one thing — how to grow rice.

In the book called *The Gullah People and Their African Heritage*, William Politzer wrote that, "hardly by chance 61 percent of the slaves brought into Charleston between 1749 and 1787 were from rich, rice-growing areas of Africa — Senegal, Gambia, Sierra Leone, and the Windward Coast. Thats because many of the people had already been slaves in their native land, they were often prepared both in attitude and in rice cultivation along the Carolina coast."

Every bit of that is just awful.

That modern Gullah Geechee are spread out on a chain of more than 100 barrier and tidal islands, usually separated from the mainland by bays or rivers. Vacationers will likely recognize some of these: Folly Island, Hilton Head, Kiawah Island, Tybee Island, Sapelo, or Jeckyll Island. Nowadays, land speculators are buying up more and more Gullah Geechee land to make more room for even more vacationers.

If you have ever been on vacation there, you've seen those tightly knit sweet grass baskets. If not, you've probably sung or heard Kumbaya at least once. If not, you've probably heard the tale of Br'er Rabbit. If you've ever experienced any of those things, thank the Gullah Geechee.

Their culture, too, certainly does still include a deep-seated belief in another plane of existence. There, harmful spirits manifest and stalk the living, sometimes to their deaths. Spirits work against the living in romance, work, and sometimes even legal affairs.

But the Gullah Geechee have spiritual weapons — honed over centuries — to combat those evil forces. Some will oversimplify and call these beliefs...superstitions. But to my mind they go well beyond simple warnings against walking under ladders, black cats, or picking up a penny on heads.

Gullah Geechee folk magic and everything it includes is, well, it's another world entirely.

Rootwork

The Gullah call it the root. It's a blend of herbalism, spiritualism, and black magic. In other places, it might be called ubia, voodoo, or Santeria.

Here's how Roger Pinckney describes the root in his book, *Blue Roots, African American Folk Magic of the Gullah People*.

He writes, "The root itself was a charm, a mojo, or gris-gris as it was known New Orleans. Most roots were cloth sacks the size of a pecan, others were liquids contained in small vials. Roots were administered or removed by a root doctor, a practitioner who, in later years, would go on to wear blue sunglasses and generally took the name of an animal. There was a Dr. Bug, a Dr. Fly, Drs. Crow, Snake, Turtle, and the infamous Dr. Buzzard."

The faithful believe that with the root, you can access supernatural forces — those on the other side of the plane — to intervene and improve your life or impair the life of someone else.

As a whole, the Gullah-Geechee spiritual tradition is an blend of Christianity, herbalism, and magic. It's been called conjuration, witchcraft, hoodoo, or rootwork. Pinckney says modern-day practitioners fear ridicule or the long arm of the law. With that, they refuse to call themselves anything at all. They simply say, "We help people."

For a good root, conjurers may use herbs, gunpowder, sulphur, salt, and candle wax. For an evil root, they'll use animal parts — crow feathers, salamander feet, a black cat's left thigh bone, and more.

Both good and evil roots may contain goofer dust, or graveyard dirt. Pinckney says if the root is intended for good, the dirt will be collected just before midnight from the grave of a righteous Christian. For evil, that dirt may be collected just after midnight from the grave of a heinous criminal.

Midnight in the garden

Wait. Did that just sound kind of familiar? *Midnight in the Garden of Good and Evil*, right? The old witchcraft lady, Minerva. Remember?

She worked some kind of magic and helped Jim Williams, the main character, out of a death sentence. To do it, she collected graveyard dirt. In the book, Minerva said the time right before midnight was the time for doing good and the time right after was for doing evil.

Minerva was inspired by a real Gullah Geechee root doctor. The book and the movie were easily the brightest lights ever shone on Gullah folk magic. But I'm not sure the book and film got it exactly right.

The book is set in Savannah, Georgia, close to the heart of Gullah Geechee country in nearby Beaufort County, South Carolina. But book and film reviews usually call Minerva a voodoo woman, or a voodoo priestess. But the Gullah tradition ain't really voodoo. It's hoodoo, or rootwork.

Voodoo is an established religion practiced largely in Africa and Haiti. Hoodoo is a sort of loose system of folk magic with no strict or formal ecclesiastical structure.

So, where'd *Midnight in the Garden of Good and Evil* get that voodoo stuff? Maybe from John Berendt, the book's author. In the book, Jim Williams, that main character, says, "If I told you Minerva was a witch doctor or a voodoo priestess, I'd be close. She was the common law wife of Dr. Buzzard, the last great voodoo practitioner in Beaufort County. Whether you know it or not, you are in the heart of voodoo country. This whole coastal area has been loaded with it since the slaves brought voodoo with them from Africa."

All right, voodoo, hoodoo. They *are* close and they rhyme. And I'm not claiming to be an expert on this stuff. Berendt did get plenty right. He called Dr. Buzzard the king of the Lowcountry root doctors. Minerva, or the character she's based upon anyway, really was Dr. Buzzard's wife, and she carried on his practice after he died.

The real Minerva and Dr. Buzzard

The *Savannah Morning News* said Valerie Fennel Aiken was the basis for the book's character, Minerva. In what you might expect, not much is known about her. She barely even let herself be photographed — only once for a movie promo and another for a story in *Time* magazine. She was afraid photographs would open her up to hexes. Aiken died in a South Carolina hospital in 2009. The cause of death was not given to the press, and her age was not known.

All right, what about that Dr. Buzzard? Pinckney calls him the "master of the shadow world," though not much is known about him, either. Certainly not the location of his final burial ground. Why not? Pinckney said "a finger or a toe bone from the famous Dr. Buzzard would be a priceless relic with enormous spiritual power."

But his real name is known, Stephany Robinson. Described in 1943, "The elderly man might have been mistaken for a bishop in the AME church. He was tall, slightly bowed, benign of expression, and soberly dressed in quality black."

But the man had a nationwide clientele of thousands. Dr. Buzzard was said to have been a courtroom specialist with the ability to tip the scales of justice with spells, hexes, and roots. He would also dispense advice, predict lottery numbers, and control spirits.

Other Gullah beliefs

These beliefs are potent in the Sea Islands and even "govern the lives" of the Gullah Geechee, Politzer wrote. Charms are worn by most to ward off evil spirits. Pennies are nailed to the doorstep for good luck. The left eye jumping means bad news. The right eye jumping means good news. A hooting owl means someone is going to die. Every itch has a magic meaning.

Witches and hags are the disembodied spirts of an old woman. They are more feared than ghosts, especially if they hold a grudge. Ghosts inhabit the living world in the in the form of animals or dwarves. Along the Sea Islands, you'll hear of beasts like boo-hags, boo-daddies, dolls, and conjure horses. Then there's the plat-eye, of course, a hideous and greatly feared one-eyed ghost. Plat-eye is also said to be a mythical monster with glowing red eyes.

Haint blue

So, what about haint blue? Consider it another one of those spiritual weapons. Haint blue is really many shades of lighter blues — think of robin's egg blue all the way to almost a deep turquoise. But those colors don't just get to be haint blue.

The baby's room is not haint blue, for example. The color only gets the distinction if it's painted outside on doors, or window trim, or, more commonly, the ceiling of a front porch.

Now, haint is a word I grew up with in the foothills of the Appalachian Mountains. It was an old-timers word for ghost. But the word also has a tradition in the Lowcountry. Somewhere along the way, the word haint met up with some Gullah folk magic, survived for generations, and made its way onto the shelves of Sherwin Williams and Benjamin Moore and into the pages of the *Washington Post* style section. But how?

Coastal plantations used to grow indigo, which was then used to make dye. Planters gave the dregs from the boiling pot to their slaves. They used it to decorate window frames and porch posts in the belief that the color kept the plentiful spirts at bay. When plantations stopped growing indigo, Gullah slaves continued the tradition using blue paint.

But why did the Gullah believed that that blue color would keep out harmful spirits? The most common idea is that the blue color resembled water and that water creates a divide between the spirit world and the living world. Some have said haints would mistake the color with the sky and pass right through the porch ceiling. Either way, the color outside the home protected the homeowner from being taken or influenced by haints.

Designers nowadays say that haint blue does more than keep away evil spirts. Some have said they've heard it called "dirt dauber blue" because the color keeps stinging insects from building nests on porches. Others say the color is just bright and helps a porch hold onto sunlight as the day fades.

But whatever the attraction, haint blue is mainstream. Hannah Yeo, the color and design expert for Benjamin Moore, told *The Washington Post* in 2017, that "blue porch ceilings have been a long-standing tradition in many parts of the Southern states for centuries. The tradition has made its way beyond the South and is influencing design across the country." Yeo said her picks for haint blue from Benjamin Moore included arctic blue, clear skies, and harbor haze.

Sherwin Williams has an entire page devoted to haint blue on its website. There, the company says haint blue can be anything from the palest of powder blues to coral and even gray. From its line, the company suggests haint blue colors of hazel, atmospheric, and pool blue.

If you want to see if a haint blue might work for your house, head on over to slideshows by *Southern Living* and *Garden and Gun*, the undisputed arbiters of Southern taste (depending on what generation you're talking to, of course). If you want to drink Haint Blue, head down to historic downtown Mobile, Alabama. There, you'll find Haint Blue Brewing Co.

I learned about haint blue on one of many visits to the South Carolina Lowcountry. The bit of research I did at the time told me that the color — painted that way — held spirits at bay and that it was generally a Southern tradition. Well, as I hope you know by now, strange tales and the American South are my peanut butter and jelly, my biscuits and gravy, my Coke and peanuts.

So, when my wife and I renovated our house a few years ago, I really only wanted one thing from the paint department. And, since then, our front porch ceiling has been a beautiful shade of robin's egg blue — a shade of haint blue — and nary a haint nor evil spirit has crossed our threshold since.

16

Crytpo Gumbo

The Wild Girl of Catahoula

The fishermen couldn't tell much about her, but they knew that she was wild.

The newspaper that carried their story about their encounter said, she wore only "nature's garments." She was covered in hair and she moved like a cat. And if that wasn't scary enough, the hunters said the girl carried a knife or a sword. And it seemed to them that she knew how to use it.

Their fear was plain. They all they all ran away from the girl and they came home with the story of the wild girl of Catahoula.

Word had gotten around that fall of 1888. But it sounded crazy. But then it sounded plausible at the same time.

Catahoula Parish was a wild patch of Louisiana. Water is everywhere in the parish untouched, untamed bayous and oxbow lakes dot the southern end of the parish. The northern end is veined with so many rivers. There's the Black River, the Tensas River Ouachita River, just to name a few.

In the north, the Boeuf Wildlife Management Area spills south into the Sicily Island Hills State Wildlife Management Area. A little further south the Catahoula National Wildlife Refuge spills south into the Dewey Wills Wildlife Management Area. All of that is just to say that Catahoula Parish is wild and it's a natural haven for wildlife. If you hunt or fish, this part of Louisiana is truly a sportsman's paradise, just like the license plate says.

You can imagine how wild it was back in 1888, when all those modern-day wildlife refuges were just wild places. They were dense and unknown...dense and unknown enough to hide just about anything that didn't want to be found.

It was in that time in one of those places that four men went fishing. They came back with a tale, one that would spark years of talk. And that talk would form a legend that Catahoula Parish still talks about today.

Like I said, stories had been circulating through the parish and and some got back to Alexandria, the seat of the parish saying a wild girl out in the woods. But most of those stories were hardly believed. A wild girl? It sounded absurd. It did until those four men got back to town with the same story.

Now, their story had a little extra meat on it, details that most of the town's folk had never heard before. But more than anything, it was the quality of the men themselves that made the wild girl real to many.

The Lake Charles Echo newspaper, said it was Captain J. M. Ball, "a large planter near here," J.C. Goulden, the "leading scenic artist," M.W. Calvert, the city marshal, and Charles Goldenberg, the bookkeeper at the Levine Lumberyard that made up the fishing party that September

"Your correspondent considered it a hoax till today, when Captain Ball came to town," reads the story.

Ball told the reporter that he was fishing, when he heard some hogs close at hand. Then, they were snuffling and squealing, like something had caught one. Ball asked Goulden, the artist, to go with him to investigate. Here's how the paper described what they saw:

"They soon came to a human being standing on a log with a pig under one arm and a short knife in the other. She was getting up on the log to avoid the hogs. When she saw the gentlemen about 30 yards off, she didn't seem half as much afraid as they did. In fact, Ball said that they started in the opposite direction first, but they were facing the creature the whole time.

"Ball said it was a white female without clothes and would seem to weigh about 140 pounds. And she was active as a cat. When they got off a little ways, she took to the bushes. Close at hand with pig and knife, Ball said she was covered with wild hair, varying in length on different parts of her body.

"Calvert, the city marshal, and Goldenberg, the bookkeeper, both said they saw the tracks of the woman and the blood of the pig and never saw two men more frightened.

"Who the strange creature is? No one can imagine. But the existence of the Wild Girl of Catahoula is no longer a matter of doubt."

A few months after this, a family said the Wild Girls cooked up one of their geese and slid back into the woods, never to be found. A few months after that a couple of hunters in LaSalle Parish said they saw the girl, said that she was frightening, but did amazing things. They they tried to talk to her but she wouldn't let him get close. They said she is as fleet as a deer. In one leap, they said, she cleared a root 7 feet high.

She uses no language only gibberish, the hunters said. They said that she was around 16 years old, 4 and-a-half feet tall with long, brown hair, and weighed around 125 to 140 pounds. She carried an old knife, they said, and seemed to limp when she walked.

New reports about the girl fired up again In 1891.

"A wild woman — supposed to be the Wild Girl of Catahoula — made her appearance in the upper portion of Franklin Parish Saturday," reads a report from New Orleans. "Those who saw her report her as being very tall, and powerful, and covered with hair and carrying a knife or a sword. Yesterday she was seen again and assaulted a boy in the neighborhood of Lamar, but was driven away by a number of people. As she seemed violent and armed, a number of men with dogs started out today to capture her."

Those men and those dogs never did catch the Wild Girl of Catahoula. No one else ever did, either.

The White River Monster

Dig around newspaper archives and you'll find a 1911 mention of a monster of the White River. Now, that long ago day a fisherman wrestled with a big catfish, he hooked on a trotline. It took him a long time but when he got it landed the fish was 74 pounds: a monster catfish.

That one was a monster, all right, but it wasn't *the* monster, the White River Monster that folks would come to know, and love, and believe in to this very day.

The city of Newport, Arkansas sits right in the corner of a big bend of the river, sending the White from flowing almost straight south to nearly northwest. Just outside of town in a deep eddy of the river, is where folks around Newport have seen what they described as an enormous boulder. It will rise to the surface of the water, a boulder that could be the back of a enormous monster the size of a boxcar.

It's unknown exactly when the White River Monster was first sighted. Some stories will even say the monster was responsible for pulling down a Union or Confederate gunboat in the Civil War, depending on what story you hear. Some say that sightings began around 1915, but they went largely unreported to newspapers or local officials.

But White River Monster mania began in Newport in 1937. That year, *Time* magazine reported that a sharecropper woman was drawing a bucket from a well. That's when she looked out over the turgid waters of the White River and saw it. She shrieked and scurried into the house after her husband, reads the magazine which didn't give the woman's name. The woman's husband popped his head out, took one look, and straightaway headed for the home of Bramlett Bateman, the owner of the plantation. The man and his wife told Bateman they'd seen a monster.

Bateman skeptically stepped over to the river and then let out a whoop. Sure enough! There *was* a monster Bateman said, and to him it was as big as a boxcar and slick as a slimy elephant without legs. Then Bateman rushed off to Newport six miles away.

It was there that Bateman must have devised a business plan. In a matter of days, he and the Newport Chamber of Commerce had planted signs all over the county: "This way to the White River Monster!" Bateman installed a fence around the viewing area and charged a 25-cent admission to see the thing.

Later that year, the White River Monster gained official interest from the Arkansas state government. The Secretary of the Arkansas Game and Fish Commission, wanted the thing — whatever it was — to be identified and then captured or destroyed.

He called for a zoologist from the University of Arkansas to head out to Bateman's farm and have a look around. A Game and Fish Commission report said the White River Monster is supposed to rise and surface in the late afternoon and it floats or swims around for periods of time from 5 to 15 minutes with its head underwater. No one has ever seen its head, the report said. It was described as being the width of an automobile and as long as three autos. The back was said to look like a wet elephant.

The eddy in which the monster supposedly made its lair was said to be 65 feet deep, deep enough, as the newspaper said, to "accommodate any sort of gar and catfish of a size to satisfy its appetite." Old timers called the deep eddy a bottomless pit.

It's unknown, really, if the state zoologist ever found anything. But later that year, a diver with United States Engineer's Office was going to solve the White River riddle for good and all. Charles

Brown was a river bottom walker. He was going to don some diving togs, arm himself with a spear, and get to the bottom of the monster story.

He'd visited Newport and talked with key eyewitnesses. But he wasn't sold on the monster story.

"Oh, I'm convinced there's something in the river, all right," Brown said told a newspaper at the time. "In my opinion, it's nothing more than a large fish, maybe a catfish. I'll find out."

Hundreds turned out to watch Brown hunt the monster. According to the story at whiterivermonster.com hundreds "lined the shore, munched on farmer Bateman's barbecued goat sandwiches and sipped his cold drinks," reads the story.

A loudspeaker was erected. And after much ado on the great morning diver Brown went down into the swirling river. He reported that visibility was only 3 inches. He came up after 75 minutes of fumbling around in there. In the afternoon, he descended again. But returned with no report. Later that night, spectators danced and had fun at a "Monster Dance," beneath flickering lamps.

Attendance fell off the next day but diver Brown descended again. When an air valve jammed in the helmet of his diving suit, he popped unexpectedly to the surface. He still hadn't seen anything. By that time, the crowds had melted completely away. Later, so didn't diver Brown.

White River Monster sightings kind of fell off over the years but they resurfaced in the summer of 1971. Many residents reported seeing flashes of its huge bulk, swirling in the dark water, reads a newspaper account.

"At the time, it was over 40 foot long and weighed weigh over a ton and it looked like it could eat anything anywhere anytime, said Newport resident, Ernest Dinks.

Another monster witness, Cloyce Warren, told the paper that it was 30-to-40 feet long, with a spiny-ridge backbone and it was splashing all around. The spiny backbone would become a Hallmark of the White River Monster from then on.

A couple of years later, the monster got some help from state officials. In 1973 the Arkansas Senate passed a resolution declaring a part of the White River near Newport as the "White River Monster sanctuary and refuge" where it "shall be unlawful to molest, kill, trample, or harm the White River Monster while in its state of retreat."

Any hardcore Harry Potter fan can tell you that the White River Monster influence did not stop in the 70s or in Arkansas or even at the American shores of the Atlantic Ocean. The monster stories inspired J.K. Rowling to include it among the magical beasts in "The History of Magic in North America" series on the Pottermore website. Here's what she says:

"Thiago Quintana, an American wand maker who worked in the early 20th century, used a single spine taken from the back of a White River Monster as the core in all his wands. This initially raised concerns of overfishing, but because Quintana was the only one who knew how to lure the creatures, it ultimately did not have very much of an ecological impact. Quintana fiercely guarded the secret to luring White River Monsters until his death, after which wands containing White River Monster spine cores were no longer made."

The Houston Bat Man

This story is obscure, obscured to history and even to many who live right there, in Houston, Texas. There's just not much known about it.

He, or it or, or whatever it was, was only seen once. Its description, didn't make much sense or even match up to anything like it at the time. Though some say, now that something like it has been seen all over Texas and Mexico.

The story that started the Houston Bat Man legend began in the early morning hours of one hot, June night. Here's how the United Press told the story at the time.

"Five persons, all of whom live in the same house, complain to police that they saw a combination of Superman and Captain Midnight perched in an oak tree outside their home early Thursday. They said he disappeared in the light of a mysterious rocket and then a second aerial display.

"Police say they were investigating the stories but admitted they were not equipped to handle such phenomena. Miss Hilda Walker, 23, accompanied by her husband, Lloyd, were the first to report the affair to authorities.

"She said it was 2:30 in the morning and because it was so hot, she and her husband and the landlady's 14-year-old daughter were all sitting on a porch when the entire yard seemed wrapped in a heavy shadow. All of a sudden this, shadow settled in the tree, Walker said. 'We all looked up and saw a bat man. He was balancing himself on a tree limb, and there was a dim, gray light all around.'

She said the creature was about 6-and-a-half feet tall, wearing a black cape and skin-tight, dark pants. He had quarter-length boots on and he looked like a white man.

'I could see him plainly and could see that he had big wings folded at his shoulders,' she said.

"Walker's husband and the young girl agree. They said the bat man perched in the tree. A few moments, they sat paralyzed and watched as a mysterious, white flame and smoke shot up behind him. Then, a burning object — like a flying paintbrush — scooted across the horizon and the bat man faded from view.

"The young girl said she got home just in time to see the flying paintbrush. Another roomer, a man of about 71, said he saw the weird, shadowy fellow in the tree. Though, he said he just merely went back in and went to bed.

The Walkers agreed it could not have been their imagination.

They said they were so shook up by the episode that they were thinking about heading back to Bryan, Texas where they had moved only three months ago."

17

Lucy of Roaring Fork

On a cold night like back in 1900, a man named Foster rode his old mare through the woods. He was headed home, passing by the Roaring Fork River just outside of Gatlinburg.

He couldn't believe his eyes. There on the secluded trail was a woman. Foster's eyes could not deny that this woman was beautiful. They also could not deny that even though it was cold, cold outside, this beautiful woman wore no shoes.

Foster was a Smoky Mountain gentleman, so he offered this mysterious woman a ride. She climbed on the back of Foster's mare and introduced herself as Lucy. She wrapped her arms tightly around Foster's waist and they rode through the dark woods. As they rode, Foster's senses tingled and his imagination ran wild. He was falling in love with this enigmatic Lucy.

They reached her home and Lucy climbed down form the horse. She thanked Foster and he said the pleasure was all his. What else would he say? Foster had already decided he'd make Lucy his bride.

He woke the next day with Lucy on his mind. He saddled that old mare and lit out for her house. He knocked on the door and found an older couple, Lucy's parents. He told of the nighttime ride and asked permission to court their fair daughter.

But all his hope and love for Lucy turned to ashes. Her parents told Foster that his Lucy had died two weeks earlier. It left Foster crestfallen and with one distributing question: if Lucy had been dead for two weeks, who was that mysterious, barefoot woman from the woods?

To this day, Smoky Mountain folks still tell of a woman spotted along the Roaring Fork Motor Nature Trail. She never speaks and she wears no shoes.

3:33 Ghost Girl

If you want a real Smoky Mountains experience, head to Le Conte Lodge. It sits way up high with breathtaking views. At 6,500 feet, the lodge is the highest guest lodge in the Eastern United States. Get up there and you'll stay in a little log cabin.

Stay up there, too, and you might meet a new friend in the middle the night. Visitors to the lodge have — for a long time — reported seeing a little ghost girl and they say she's punctual. The stories say that guests will wake with the feeling they're being watched. They'll rise at 3:33 a.m. and see this dark, little girl sitting on the end of their bed.

Greenbrier Lodge Ghost

There's another lodge up in the Smokies with another ghost. This is one is a bit more frightful than the little 3:33 Ghost Girl, though.

The story goes that a woman, Lydia, was staying at the Greenbrier Lodge, now call the Greenrbrier Restaurant. She was young and in love with a young man who lived around Gatlinburg and they are to be married.

Lydia rose at the Greenbrier on the day of her wedding. She slipped her beautiful white wedding gown over her head and rode into town to meet her love at the altar inside the church there in town. But, there at the altar, Lydia would wait. For hours she waited but her her lover never showed.

Finally, Lydia was coaxed from the church and back up the

mountain to the Greenbrier. She tried to be brave but her emotions got the best of her. Lydia found a rope and tied a noose. She headed up the stairs to a balcony on the Greenbrier's second floor.

She slung the rope over a rafter beam, tightened the noose around her neck, and jumped. She swayed softly side to side for all the guests to see, her white wedding dress hanging limply toward the floor.

Lydia never knew what became of her fiancee. Maybe she figured he got cold feet. Maybe he didn't love her in the first place. If either were true, he'd humiliated Lydia in front of everybody. But neither were true.

If Lydia had known the truth, she may have still ended up at the end of that rope. Days after Lydia killed herself at the Greenbrier, her fiancée was found in the woods, mauled to death by a mountain cat.

Some say Lydia's spirit takes the form of a cat and exacts revenge. An old caretaker said his night rounds were troubled with a voice repeating "mark my grave, mark my grave." Knowing where Lydia was buried he climbed down the mountains and did what she asked. He marked her grave and heard the voices no more.

Many guests say they can still see Lydia — still wearing her white wedding dress — wandering the halls of the Greenbrier.

Wheatlands Plantation

All through the Smokies, you're going to find little, rustic cabins. But down in Sevierville, you can find a bona fide mansion and it is bona fide haunted.

It's the Wheatlands Plantation house, named for its large annual wheat harvests brought in with slave labor. The land was the site of battles in the Civil War and Revolutionary War.

It was also the site of the Battle of Boyd's Creek. In it, white settlers fought a band of Cherokee, killing 28 warriors. They were buried on the site in a mass grave that now sits directly behind Wheatlands Plantation house.

If battles, slave oppression, and the massacre of dozens of Cherokee weren't enough to fuel hauntings at the site, it is said that Wheatlands Planation house saw 70 deaths within its walls.

For all of it, guests report a number of strange encounters. The ghosts of the original Wheatlands family are seen often, still dressed as if it were 1830. The spirits of two women have been seen on the mansion's staircase. Both of them reportedly died on the stairs, one from a heart attack and another broke her neck in a fall there.

The parlor floorboards are still stained with the blood of a father slain by his son. These stains keep appearing even though they've been cleaned many times. Visitors say they can sometimes hear the yells of a man, followed by thuds that sound like a body hitting the floor. Then, they report a disgusting gurgling sound, almost like the murder is on a continuous playback loop.

18

Mississippi Gulf Coast

Piracy by night

The pirates rowed toward the deserted island in the cover of night. The sea there was calm and black as as pitch. It lapped gently around the rowboat only stirred by the pirates' oars. The boat crew was small, handpicked by the captain to move the treasure chest.

From the stern, the captain kept an eye on the sparse stand of palm trees on the island ahead. He could just make out the shaggy palm fronds swaying ever so slightly against the starry sky. He was a hard man, a fact proved true by the amount of gold in that treasure chest. Pirate captains had to be strong and ruthless and he was.

That's why his men followed him. Sure, they could handle the insults and the barked orders from the captain if it meant one day they'd go home with their fair share of the gold inside that chest.

That night, they aimed to bury that gold in a place no one would think to look. And no one, they thought, would ever come looking here. It was a deserted barrier island right off the coast of Mississippi. As far as pirate dens went, this one was off the beaten trail. That's likely why the pirate captain chose it.

The boat's keel kneaded into the island's soft sand. The captain jumped from the bow and began striding up the beach. The men stowed the oars, scrabbled over the gunwales, and hoisted that treasure chest over the surf.

They followed the captain to a clearing, not far from the boat. Surely, this was not where the captain intended to bury their hard-won treasure. The pirates paused, thunked the chest onto the sand, and the captain began to speak.

Only he and one other man would bury this treasure, he said. That would leave only two men alive to know exactly where it was hidden. Secrecy was security. The captain called for a volunteer. Silence. The only sounds were the waves lapping at the shore and the air riffling through the sea oats. The men shot nervous glances at each other. The silence stretched out uncomfortably.

One pirate, finally, cleared his throat, raised his hand, and stepped forward. Maybe he thought his volunteered help would win him favor with the captain and, perhaps, a bigger share of the gold in the chest. Another thought flicked through his mind but he batted it away before it showed on his face. What if the captain died? Only he would know the location of the gold. Secrecy was security after all.

The pirate captain smiled, nodded, laid a shovel over his shoulder, and cocked his head at the chest. The man glanced at his crew mates with a smirk, grabbed one of the chest's handles, and the captain grabbed the other. Together, they began walking into the thicket just beyond the beach.

The man could barely see the captain through the brush and the darkness. But he could hear him, rustling just ahead of him through the pine trees and orchard grass. The sounds stopped and the pirate found himself in a small, sandy clearing.

They lowered the chest to the sand and the man looked around. The captain said nothing but pointed to the very center of the alcove. He leaned against a tree, crossed his arms, and waited. The pirate's shovel bit into the ground. He scooped endless spades of sand over his shoulder. More than once he thought how much quicker the work would go if the captain brought a shovel for himself but he dared not to give the opinion a voice.

Finally, the captain bid the man to halt when his hole had him up to the shoulders. He climbed out of the pit, laid the shovel aside, and looked down into his work. The caption nodded his approval. The pair grabbed the chest, lowered it as far as they could, and released it to the bottom with a final thud. The pirate quickly filled the hole, scattering the excess sand, and smoothed the ground, leaving no trace of a hole or a pirate treasure chest.

Pleased with the deed, the captain laughed and shook the man's hand. Now he was sure he had the captain's favor and a bit more of his share of the gold. His good feeling took away any of those earlier thoughts of cold-blooded murder.

Still laughing, the captain bid the man to take a knee before him. Surely this was some sort of pirate ritual of which the man had never heard. He'd never buried a treasure before. Maybe feeling like a knight in a storybook, the man fell to one knee, and bowed his head before his commander.

In one fluid motion, the captain skinned his sword, raised it high over his head with two hands, brought it down upon the man's neck, and cut his head clean off his body. Secrecy is security after all.

The poor pirate was dead. Left to guard that old treasure chest. Some say he still does to this very day.

Another terrifying fishing tale

Centuries later, two fishermen rowed toward the deserted island in the cover of night.

The sea there was calm and black as as pitch. It lapped gently around the rowboat, only moved to foam around the oars pulled hard by the fishermen. From the stern, they kept an eye on the sparse stand of palm trees on the island ahead. One could just make out the shaggy palm fronds swaying ever so slightly against the starry sky.

The bow kneaded the soft sand as they made the shore. They hopped over the gunwales, grabbed their gear, their food, and their catch. They settled in on a spot on the beach near some palmetto bushes.

They cooked fish and made coffee over the campfire. The cozy light beat back that dense dark that laid all around them and the island. For a time, they could relax and enjoy the environs of Deer Island.

Then, something rustled in the bushes nearby. It was a wild hog, had to be. What else was out here? But there was no grunting, no squealing. But it was something. Something big had to make that kind of racket. But there was nothing to do but keep their eyes open and alert.

In a flash, their heads turned at the same moment. Something big burst through the palmettos. That's all they knew at first, that it was big. Because the rest of it made no sense at all. This thing before them was a human skeleton with no skull.

On hands and feet, the fishermen scrabbled backwards through the sand just to put a few feet between this headless skeleton and their own safety. They didn't want to see this thing but they couldn't look away either.

It groped toward them in an awkward, dead, sickening kind of motion. That was enough. The fishermen found their feet, left their campfire burning, and left all their gear beside it. They ran down the beach, shoved their boat into the water, hopped in, and began paddling in the only direction that made sense — away from Deer Island.

In the light of the next day, those fishermen returned. The island beamed almost happily in the sunshine, the direct opposite of its foreboding and even horrific guise from the night before.

They beached their boat on the same spot and walked the exact same route they'd walked only hours before. They carefully picked their way through the sea oats, keeping their eyes up on the island ahead of them, alert for any dangers.

They found their campsite. Everything was just as they'd left it, except their fire: dead, charred, and ashy but still slightly warm. They looked around and found the spot where the headless skeleton — "That's what it was, right?" they asked each other. "Am I crazy or did you see it, too?" — had burst from the bushes.

The sea breeze had removed traces of any tracks. Even if they found some, they probably would not have followed them. They stowed their gear, hauled it back to the boat, and paddled out, once again, away from Deer Island.

This story spread like wildfire across the Mississippi Gulf Coast. Deer Island is a stone's throw from Biloxi, easily visible every single day right across the bay. Once upon a time, folks lived out there on Deer Island but not many. For most of the time anyone could remember, it was deserted. With no one around the bring any news from the island, anything could be happening out there, even headless skeletons jumping out of the bushes.

The fishermen's story fueled a new curiosity about Deer Island. Before long, many a bold youth would lead expeditions to its shores. They'd hunt around for signs of the fishermen's camp site and tramp through bushes, hoping to find that headless skeleton. No one ever found it but more than a few Biloxians have said they've seen this thing, whatever it is.

The only solid proof of anything at all was the discovery of some old coins found not far from the fishermen's campsite. This gold was old. Whatever inscriptions were once there had been smoothed out over decades until they were unreadable.

But this puzzle piece fit neatly with that old Deer Island pirate story told for centuries before. Many on the coast believe that, maybe, the headless skeleton was that unfortunate pirate volunteer. Remember he agreed to bury the treasure and the captain had his head for it? Secrecy is security, remember? It's said that headless pirate volunteer still protects the treasure of Deer Island years and years after his death.

Cahill Haunted Mansion

Many were relieved when the old Cahill House burned. It had been magnificent. Built in 1915, it was a stately three-story, wood-frame mansion. And it stood in the affluent Handsboro neighborhood of Gulfport. There, it backed up to the beautiful Bayou Bernard. But over the years the house had fallen into disrepair. Its owners — Dr. Kendall Gregory and his wife, Ginny — planned to just have it torn down. They just couldn't stay there anymore and left.

Whatever damage was started by neglect, was finished by Hurricane Camille. After that, the Cahill House was uninhabitable. Windows were blown out and covered over with wood panels. Litter was strewn across the grown-over front yard, left to go wild in the absence of the Gregory family. They tried to hire crews to pull the house down but all the crews were all busy cleaning up other properties in the storm's aftermath. So, the Cahill House was left to rot, to molder on the bank of the bayou.

For a year, the vacant property stood, its shabby appearance and cobwebs giving it every cliche detail of a real haunted house. But that reputation came not only from its look. Every Coastal Mississippi kid new the stories of the Cahill House, the ghost stories.

Stories start somewhere, right? Well, most of the stories from Cahill House came from Ginny Gregory herself. She said creepy feelings and creepy things began almost as soon as they moved in. "I felt like I was always being watched," she said.

One night her son's college friends were sleeping in an upstairs bedroom. They woke to what sounded like footsteps running through the room. Another night in that same in that same room, her son woke to see what looked like a little boy walking out of the closet. He walked through the room and out the door. The son rose, ran across the room, and out into the hall. But there was no one to be seen.

That same son was once asleep on a couch in the den. At around 4:30 a.m., he saw another small child in the room. Only this one was luminous, he said. It seemed to glow into the darkness. The figure of the small child got larger as it passed through the room until it reached the far window. There, it poofed out of existence. Another time, her son laid his school jacket across the kitchen table. It suddenly burst into flames.

Maybe the most troubling story of the Cahill House that Ginny told happened on the day in 1963 when President John F. Kennedy was assassinated in Dallas, Texas. She said her children woke that morning, walked downstairs, but found something unusual about the light shining through the window. The drapes and the window had been smeared with something. It looked like blood, though no one had been injured. Ginny's husband, Dr. Gregory, took samples from the window and confirmed it was, indeed, blood, human blood. Though no one could explain how it might have gotten there.

All of these bigger, blockbuster stories were punctuated with smaller events, usually sounds heard frequently around the house. The family would hear footsteps running up and down stairs. They'd hear moaning and screaming at all hours. It was enough that Ginny bought ear plugs so she wouldn't have to hear the sounds anymore.

For years, the folks around the Mississippi Coast heard these stories. So, after Hurricane Camille — in the summer of 1969 — they went to see for themselves. In the absence of the Gregory family — the property owners — bold teenagers might dare each other to stand in the driveway at night. Maybe some got bold enough to climb up on the porch, knock on the door, and run away.

Later, though, local kids were breaking into the Cahill House, hoping to catch a glimpse of a spirit or, maybe just for bragging rights. Then, it got worse for the house. Items were taken, fixtures were torn from walls, junk was strewn over every floor, and someone splashed a pail of red paint over the walls. It was said the house had been viciously vandalized.

By late summer and early fall that year, more and more people — especially grown folks — began showing up at the Cahill House. The *Biloxi Sun Herald* newspaper said "ghost mania had spread to adults in the community." A visit to the haunted house had just become a thing to do. The curious showed up by the dozens, especially around nightfall. For this, the home's wealthy neighbors complained to police and tried to shoo off the onlookers with "no trespassing" signs posted around their property.

But the Gregories just let the onlookers come. Not only that, they began to allow — and even invite — paranormal researchers into the house for investigations and seances. One of these was Dr. David Bubar. He was a Baptist minister from Memphis who claimed to be a psychic, a medium, and a predictor of the future.

In one of his investigations of the Cahill House, Bubar was joined by about 20 people. He put himself into a trance. Channeling a spirit from beyond, Bubar revealed the alleged dark history of the house. The stories were of murder, the murder of women and children in an upstairs bathroom. He told of young women brought in from Louisiana who were used and abused in the home.

At one point, Bubar channeled a spirit named "Flossie." Through Bubar, Flossie said, "there were candles in the kitchen. I meant to the burn the place up. I have got to get rid of this place."

Flossie's story lines up with another story about the house Ginny had often told. She said she came in from shopping one day and opened the cabinet under the sink. There, she found a little, red candle that was lit and glowed softly in the darkness. Upset, Ginny called her maid and accused her of trying to burn the house down.

But the maid fired back, "Someone is trying to get me," and explained that the same thing had happened to her not long before.

Whether Bubar knew this story before he conjured Flossie during that seance, is unknown. If he did, it could have fit with his reputation as a charlatan. If not, the similarities in the story are worth a closer look.

With Flossie's story and whatever other intuition Dr. Bubar might have had, he predicted at the seance that the Cahill House would burn one day.

Again, the Gregory family had opened the home to paranormal researchers just like Bubar. So, months after his prediction about the house, another group — a different group — was holding a seance in the haunted house in Handsboro.

The newspapers did not know nor report the names of those holding that seance in the house that Friday night. The last known persons — four of them — left the house at about 1 a.m. Later, a truck was seen by neighbors at around 2:30 a.m. Whatever happened, the paper said flames erupted in the Cahill House at around 1:20 p.m. on that Saturday afternoon.

Here's how the *Sun Herald* reported the story:

"The state fire Marshall has been summoned to investigate a fire which nearly destroyed an old residence on Kimball Drive in Handsboro Saturday afternoon, a once-elite, three-story house long suspected by many to be haunted.

"Flames erupted on the second story of the frame structure about 1:20 p.m. and quickly engulfed the building, where, ironically, a 'seance' had been held the night before.

"The seance, held Friday night by four local residents with the Gregories' permission, was reportedly interrupted several times by curiosity seekers, but no trouble was noted.

"Gulfport Fire Superintendent Hugh Haynie said at the scene of the fire that the 'suspicious nature' of the blaze will necessitate an investigation by the state fire marshall to determine the nature of the fire."

This fire was big news. The story was pushed to A1 above the fold in the Sunday edition of the *Sun Herald*. Now, the fire was news, but the home's haunted past was the news hook. The headline read, "Cahill House Destroyed; Spirits Free?"

In a phone interview after the blaze, Dr. Bubar said he was "delighted that place has burned down as it will free those poor, unfortunate entities that have been trapped there."

Later in his life, Bubar would predict another fire, a big one. His prediction was true. But that's mainly because he helped to start the fire himself. But that's a story for another time.

The Singing River

Some say the Pascagoula River....sings.

For hundreds of years visitors and locals alike have visited the river to hear it and have tried to describe this eerily beautiful sound. Some have said it sounds like a flute or the sound a glass can make when you rub a finger along its rim. Others have said the sound is like a mysterious humming or a metallic buzzing. Either way, this sound is the way the Pascagoula River earned its nickname. Folks simply call it the Singing River.

The river is wild. That's on purpose. The Pascagoula is about 80 miles long. It starts in southeastern Mississippi, runs south, through Escatawpa and Moss Point, and flows into the Mississippi Sound at Gautier and, then, into the Gulf of Mexico. At no point does it meet a dam or hardly any man made thing at all. It is truly wild.

Like so many Southern stories, there are many versions of the sound's origin. Some include mermaids or sirens, luring the curious to the river bank only to kill them. But the prevailing story involves a dispute among two Native American tribes. That story says the Biloxi and Pascagoula tribes had co-existed along the Mississippi

Coast for generations. The Pascagoula were peaceful. The Biloxi were warriors.

A Biloxi princess was set to marry a chieftain named Otanga. However, her family had visited the Pascagoula tribe. During the visit, she met a man named Altama and fell in love with him. She broke her betrothal to Orange, and left her tribe to live with the Pascagoula to be with Altama. This angered her people and led to war. Altama, the Pascagoula who had been left by the princess, offered himself up to end the violence.

His people would not forsake him. So, as he walked into the Pascagoula to die at hand of the Biloxi and, maybe stop the fighting, others followed him. Women and children and war chiefs alike walked into the river after their leader.

As they walked, they sang, the story goes. They patterned their footsteps in a rhythm and sang a solemn requiem until the water drowned their final voice. It is said the sound of the Pascagoula River — the Singing River — are the final sounds of the that peaceful people. Go down to the banks of the Pascagoula on the Mississippi Coast and see if you can hear them for yourself.

19

Flatwoods Monster

Friday night football interrupted
They were just playing football.
It was Ed May, Freddie May, Neil Nunley, and Tommy Hyer. They were playing two-a-side ball best they could over at the big, green-grass field at Flatwoods Elementary School.
It was the middle of September 1952 and the warm breeze rising through the valley hissed through the leafy trees. The football field might've been the flattest part of Flatwoods, a secluded holler in West Virginia, nestled in the timbered hills of the Appalachian Mountains.
For the boys, though, it was just home. And it was Friday, nearing dark so school was over for the week, and Friday night, well, Friday night was the beginning of the weekend's sweet, sweet promise. Playing football with your friends like that, it has a way to shrink the world down to its purest and best elements. The past and the future were set aside and the only time that mattered were those anxious seconds between hiking the ball and — if you did it right — curling a perfect spiral right into your buddy's hands. And speaking of buddies? Shoot, they were right there. Who needed anything else? All of this is just to say that the four boys were safe and happy.
But what happened next would change everything. Not just for

the four boys and the two others they'd get involved to help them. But it would change the whole town of Flatwoods and, maybe, change how many people around there would think about the world and the universe beyond it.

A strange light in the sky drew the eyes of those four boys to the heavens. While a strange light in the sky is weird enough, it was not — by far — the weirdest thing that would happen that September Friday in Flatwoods, West Virginia. That light proved to be only the beginning of what has gone down as one of the strangest nights anywhere. That night is the reason the city limits sign there now reads "Welcome to Flatwoods, Home of the Green Monster."

Braxton County — home of Flatwoods — sits in the geographic center of West Virginia. That means it is perfectly surrounded by rolling hills of thick woods veined by rivers and dotted with two beautiful lakes. The town is about an hour northeast of Charleston, the state capitol.

Flatwoods isn't big. The city had 260 people in 2020. That was the last time the government sent anyone down there to check. But all kinds of people find their way to Braxton County, especially those who love the outdoors. Motorcycle riders flock there to take in the scenic loop trails that snake up and down the twisty mountain roads. Boaters can float canoes and kayaks through the tiny towns, farmland, and thick woods that dot the Elk River. And just about anybody can find some fun — either boating, fishing, or swimming — on Sutton Lake or Burnsville Lake.

But, believe it or not, the biggest draw in Braxton County is the paranormal. Officials there lead with the weird stuff on the county's official tourism website. It invites you to meet the Green Monster, of course. But it also points you to the haunted Haymond House and the haunted Elk Resort. If that's enough, tourism officials will help you find Bigfoot, spotted around the banks of Sutton Lake.

Back at the football field that September night in 1952, those four boys locked eyes on that strange light. It was oval shaped and looked like it was on fire as it streaked across the night sky, they said. Unable to explain what they were seeing and, maybe, carrying a bit of fear in their gut, they did what most would do. They ran home.

At the May house, Ed and Freddie told their mama that they saw a flying saucer slip across the sky and land on C.B. Fisher's nearby farm. Kathleen May was no UFO expert or police officer or anything. She was a beautician and ran her salon right there out of her house. But acting in her official capacity as a worried mother, she believed her sons enough to leave the house and climb the nearby ridge to see just what had agitated her children and their friends.

Along the way, the group added another young friend, Ronnie Shaver, and 17-year-old Eugene Lemon, a West Virginia National Guardsmen. The sky over Flatwoods that Friday night was growing dark so they all grabbed flashlights before the seven of them (and a dog) set off up the hill.

Maybe they all laughed at first. Maybe they thought this was a fun diversion, something to talk about at school or the beauty shop. Maybe they all joked as they made their way up the hill to have a look over at whatever it was that streaked across the sky and landed in C.B. Fisher's pasture. But with the flick of a flashlight, all of the humor drained, leaving only terror to fill its place.

There was an odd pulsing light, and a low hiss, and something smelled awful. They looked in awe at a giant, metallic ball sitting right there in the field in front of them. Kathleen May said they were all frozen in their tracks. Gene Lemon, the National Guardsmen, thought he'd spotted a pair of shining eyes glinting through the dark down at them from a nearby tree. He beamed his flashlight up at the eyes, expecting an owl or a possum.

Instead, they saw what they described as a fire-breathing, man-like monster, 10 feet tall with spindly arms, claw-like hands, and a bright green body that seemed to glow. Its face was round as a basketball and blood red, they said. It was enveloped in something — maybe a kind of helmet — that curved out on the sides and curved to a sharp point on top, just like the ace of spades.

Some sort of strong, sickening, metallic odor filled the air and stung their nostrils. Later, they'd all blame this odor — and whatever it came from — for a bout of nausea that had them all fainting and throwing up for the rest of the night.

Kathleen said the monster came for them with an odd bouncing, floating motion, like a sort of duckwalk. They screamed, turned tail, and ran as fast they could back down the hill to the safety of Flatwoods.

Amid those shrieks and screams, and that pulsing light of orange and green, the search party found what they were looking for and got way more than they bargained for.

"It looked worse than Frankenstein," Kathleen said at the time. "It could not have been human."

Alright, those are the basic details of the story, the details printed in newspapers across the country at the time. Few other details really exist (for the curious public anyway). But a couple of other versions of the story, one from a second-hand witness and the other from the government give a few more and we'll get to those later. But it's these basic details from the original group that form the legend of the Flatwoods Monster that would ring out of Braxton County for what is now more than 70 years.

While this story is celebrated now and spans seven decades, don't go thinking that anyone other than the seven people in the original search party immediately believed in this thing.

Back at home, word of the monster spread quickly. Within 30 minutes of the group's return, an armed posse was organized. It was led by A. Lee Stewart, a newspaper man, from nearby Sutton. Stewart experienced some of it himself and he found it hard to explain away immediately. Here's what he reported in the newspaper:

"It was about 7:15 [p.m.] when this meteorite or something was supposed to have been seen that I wandered down the street and people told me about having seen it. Then, a little while later, a call comes in from Flatwoods, about five miles away.

"Mrs. Kathleen May and six boys had gone up the hill to where the thing had supposedly landed. They could see flashes of light — flash, flash, flash, three or four times — coming from the top of the hill.

"As they kind of eased around the little bend in the road, there, in the shadows, they saw a pair of eyes. There was a peculiar odor, a very sickening hot, stuffy-smelling odor.

"The oldest boy — he's 17 — threw a flashlight on it. All the rest of them saw it, too. The boy fell backwards and all the people took to their heels and came running back to town.

"They said it was about 11 or 12 feet tall and had a shiny, metallic kind of face and protruding eyes. Its body was green. It had outstretched hands, sort of claw looking hands.

"When they got back to town, they gave the older boy a dose or two of smelling salts, and called police."

Stewart said state police weren't answering the phone that Friday night. But he tagged along with the sheriff and some deputies to have a look around that next morning. They took Gene Lemon, the 17-year-old National Guardsman with them. But Stewart said the boy had to be coaxed back up the hill and that he had to keep his hand on his shoulder the whole time and that the boy "shook and shook like he was scared to death."

At the top of the tangled and rugged hill, they did not find a meteorite or any signs one had crashed there.

The metallic odor was still there, lingering softly. Stewart said he found two places — six to eight feet in diameter — where the brush had been trampled down. There were two tracks on the ground that looked like skid marks, abut a foot wide and a car length apart. However, he said no one could possibly get a car up that hill.

"I know all these people," Stewart said. "I tried every way to tear this story down. But they all told the same story and they all stuck to it.

"I've never seen people in more fright. I'm not sure what they saw but they saw something on that hill.

"I hate to say I believe it, but I hate to say I don't believe it. Those people were scared — badly scared, and I sure smelled something."

The West Virginia State Police were finally contacted. They went up the mountain and had a look around. But they said they had no explanation for the unearthly monster, or "the thing" as they called it. But they laughed the thing off as hysteria, claiming the so-called monster had grown from seven feet to 17 feet in 24 hours. But it's not known, exactly, who made those claims.

No one could doubt that odd things were happening in the skies over West Virginia that summer night. Local police were out, looking for an airplane reported to have crashed somewhere in the vicinity of Flatwoods. Reports from several nearby states claimed a meteor, or something, was streaking across the starry sky. For many, these things explained much of what seen on that hilltop in Flatwoods.

The town's mayor, J. Holt Byrne, said he believed this "monster" was nothing more than "vapor" from that meteor. He said the meteor likely explained both the boys' "flying saucer" report and the "metallic odor" that permeated the hilltop. It's not known, exactly, how the mayor knew this, if he'd ever seen or smelled a meteor up close.

The original party stood strong on their story, suffering jokes and ridicule from many around Flatwoods. Many around there had their own theories. But theories and stories were not enough. The Flatwoods Monster caught the attention of some high-ranking military officials. And no matter what anyone thought of the story — silly or wild-eyed — the U.S. government wanted its own answers and they wanted them kept top secret.

Official interest

1952 was a busy year for the United States Air Force. The Korean War was on, of course. But a segment of the Air Force was busy stateside on a mission kept secret from American civilians. Project Blue Book cranked up in March 1952, headquartered at Wright-Patterson Air Force Base in Ohio. The project had two goals: to determine whether or not UFOs posed a national security threat and to scientifically analyze data related to UFOs.

Blue Book wasn't some fly-by-night operation cooked up by a curious commander with some serious pull. The federal government had already investigated the UFO phenomena with two previous projects, Project Sign in 1947 and Project Grudge in 1948.

In 1952, the same year the Flatwoods Monster was reported, Project Blue Book logged more than 1,500 reports of UFO activity in American skies. Warplanes were scrambled to chase flying saucers that buzzed Washington, D.C. on two consecutive weekends. In July, airmen at Patrick Air Force Base reported that seven amber-red objects silently approached restricted air space. Project Blue Book said the Flatwoods incident concluded the summer's flying saucer "panic" that had seemingly gripped the nation.

The Air Force studied the heck out of the Flatwoods case. But not much of the official investigation can be found in the Blue Book report. But it does have the narrative report taken from Neil Nunley, one of the boys who saw the monster. His testimony was taken by Air Force officials two days after the incident. Here's the report on Nunley's story:

"A huge globular mass was observed first. Down over the other side of the hilltop to the right about 50 feet away. Like a big ball of fire.

"One witness, a boy named Neil Nunley, said it seemed to dim and brighten at regular intervals. He didn't know how large it was. Some said it was big as a house. It is not clear whether a complete sphere was seen or a hemisphere resting on the ground.

"Nunley heard no noise. Others said it made a low thumping or beating sound like someone hitting on canvas. And there was another noise, halfway between a hiss and the noise made by a jet plane.

"Distracted by the globular mass, they did not see a huge figure standing to their left. One said he thought he saw animal eyes in the tree and flashed his light on them.

"Fifteen feet away, towering over their heads, was a vast shape something like a man. The face, everyone agreed, was round and blood red. No one noticed anything like a nose or a mouth. They did see eyes, or eye-like openings from which projected greenish-orange beams of light. These light beams pierced through the haze pervading the scene. In the excitement, some of the group thought the beams of light were focused upon them. Nunley was specific that they were not. They went out over their heads.

"The 'monster' could not have been more than 15 feet tall for it was under the overhanging limb of a tree and the limb was of that height.

"Originally, the group said a strange, nauseous odor resembled burning metal or burning sulphur. Under questioning, none could remember having encountered anything similar. It was finally described only basically as sickening, irritating to the throat and nasal passages. It seemed to grip you in the throat and suffocate you, they said.

"Nunley was definite about the thing's movement, although other accounts conflicted. They said it was moving toward them but, according to Nunley, it was moving in an arc, coming toward them but circling them at the same time. His description indicated the "monster" was following a circular path, which would take it back to the globe.

"When asked to walk around the room where he was being interviewed and to imitate the movement, he said that was impossible. I couldn't move as it did, he said. It just moved. It didn't walk. It moved evenly. It didn't jump.

"The witnesses departed immediately upon sighting the "monster" and no other observations were made."

As our group from Flatwoods was climbing that hill in September, UFO sightings poured into the Air Force from all over the Southeast, especially West Virginia and Virginia. Like many of those in Flatwoods, Project Blue Book officials blamed the sightings on a meteor. However, no meteor showers were predicted that night by astronomers. The monster, Air Force officials said, was "probably the glowing eyes or body of some mundane creature of the woods." They also noted that what they called "civilian saucer investigators" rejected the government's explanation.

No one will ever agree about — or ever know, really — just what the Flatwoods Monster was. But one thing that all the groups — the government, flying saucer folk, and the people of Braxton County — will agree on, is that the monster is now enshrined in West Virginia history.

For proof of this, Project Blue Book even pointed to a ballad about the monster written at the time:

The size of the phantom was a sight to behold
Green eyes and red face, so the story was told
It floated in air with fingers of flame
It was gone with a hiss just as quick as it came
Oh, phantom of Flatwoods from moon or from Mars
Maybe from God and not from the stars
Please tell us why you fly over our trees
The end of the world or an omen of peace?

Flatwoods Monster legacy

No one knows just how powerful the Flatwoods Monster story is better than Kathleen May. She was the sole adult in the witness party that night back in 1952. This made her more believable than the young boys who saw the thing, too, even the teenaged National Guardsman. So, when people over the years wanted to hear the story again, they turned to Kathleen.

In 1973, the monster incident was just over 20 years old. At the time, Kathleen told a reporter, "I just don't like to discuss it anymore. I get sick of it. Never a week goes by that someone doesn't contact me about it, either by phone or letter."

But she was a bit more open when a news reporter was writing about the 25th anniversary of the sighting.

"I still think about it occasionally, especially when I see something on television or read something in a book," she said. "With this new space program, it all fits the puzzle."

Kathleen passed away in 2009 at the age of 89. She's buried in the Flatwoods Cemetery. Her obituary mentioned her trip up the the side of that hill that Friday night in September back in 1952.

Her obituary also said the town still celebrates the phenomena of the Flatwoods Monster and the town still does. That spade-headed, green-bodied monster is one of the first things your likely to see when you Google Braxton County, West Virginia. Some around there call the monster "Braxxie," shorthand for the "Braxton County Monster" and, like I said, the city limits sign calls it the "Green Monster."

If you go to Braxton County, you can find and sit in (and Instagram) a whole series of "monster chairs." These massive wooden chairs were scattered all over the county by the Braxton County Convention and Visitors Bureau in 2015. Once upon a time, you could post your photos with the chairs and the tourism folks would send you a free Braxxie sticker.

If you want to dig deeper into the Flatwoods Monster story, you'll want to head to Downtown Sutton. There you'll find the Flatwoods Monster Museum. It houses monster collections, historical artifacts from the time, pictures, books, and more. Admission is free but you'll not want to leave without spending some money on a monster t-shirt, sticker, or a shot glass.

If all this monster hunting has you hungry, you'll want to find The Spot. The monster-themed restaurant has a big sign out front featuring two people running away from the monster. The faces of the people have been cut out for tourists photos. At The Spot, you can get a bacon sandwich called "The Encounter," a pizza calzone called "Area 51," a grilled chicken sandwich called "The Roswell," and, of course, a ham, salami, and pepperoni sandwich called "The Flatwoods."

20

The Witch of Pungo

A ducking

It had come to this.

Years of rumor. Years of odd looks. Years of sideways glances as she walked through the village. Years of unease. Name calling. Insane stories. Allegations. They'd all spurred a dozen or so court cases going back and forth. Despite all this tension, the woman never left, never backed down.

At that thought, she might've leaned back in the little boat, leaned her head back and scanned the sky. From where she sat in the bow, maybe she shook her head, for that was about all she could move. *Why didn't I just leave Pungo? Why didn't I just leave this little community and these little people? Why didn't I just leave my home on the Muddy Bank?*

A life somewhere else might've been different. It might've led her somewhere else, to some other fate. Not tied up with a scratchy length of rope that cut into her ankles and wrists. Not about to face the cold waters of the Lynnhaven River.

But her life in Pungo must have been precious to her, to live through all that. Maybe she looked down at her bound hands and feet and thought about the good things. She thought of growing up here. Thought of her father, showing her how to tend to livestock and crops. She thought of the women in her family who'd taught her how to grow herbs and how to mix them to heal others. She thought of her sons, growing up around her and learning how to survive and thrive on the Chesapeake Bay and the Atlantic Ocean. Oh, her sons, she might've thought. For them to see her like this.

But you should've heard the stories. To hear her neighbors tell it, she could conjure up storms and kill livestock with her special powers, supernatural powers. Her witch powers.

It all seemed crazy to her, ethereal even. The stories were plucked out of thin air, wrapped around her, and made real by religious fervor that was fueled with jealousy and distrust. As she sat on that boat, looking back on Pungo, the little town she loved, she could feel that fervor — those stories made real. They burned in her skin every time she moved her wrists or ankles under that scratchy rope.

The leaders in Pungo ordered a trial for the woman. The husky men at the town square tied her tightly with rope, some say from her thumbs to her toes. They hoisted her up and hauled her body to the boat and paddled out to a deep spot on the Lynnhaven.

This trial had no human judge, jury, nor executioner. The woman's fate lay inside her. Either the pure water would consume her and she'd be innocent. Or, it would reject her — she would float — and everyone would know she was in league with the devil.

With this trial, the town folk around what would become Virginia Beach, Virginia aimed to prove that Grace Sherwood was a witch. Just like they'd said all along. That trial in 1706 was the last such witch trial in Virginia history. It also made real the legend of the Witch of Pungo.

Virginia Beach

Virginia Beach, Virginia holds an insanely happy world record. It has more miles of pleasure beaches than any other place on the globe. The city lies in southeast Virginia, just north of the North

Carolina border, right where the Chesapeake Bay flows into the Atlantic Ocean.

Tourists flock to Virginia Beach every year, staying at one of the 73 hotels that sit right on the water front. That's not to mention the dozens of other hotels there crowded by visitors every year who want to surf, fish, shop, swim, sunbathe, or soak up American history.

In Virginia Beach, you can move forward at the Virginia Museum of Contemporary Art. Or, you can go back to Cape Henry, where English colonists — who would go on to found Jamestown — first sat foot on what is now American soil.

Virginia Beach is a bright, friendly American city with natural and cultural treasures for the world to see. But head up to the city's attic. Dig through the boxes in the corner and you might find that witch.

The witch

No one thought Grace White was a witch when she married James Sherwood in the spring of 1680. She'd grown up Pungo, right around where she and her new husband built their home on the bank of Muddy Creek, just south of modern-day Virginia Beach.

Her relatives taught her how to be a good citizen and a good member of the Lynnhaven Parish Church. From her mother, Grace learned how to be a healer. She learned to use herbs to cure animals and treat her ailing neighbors. She learned to be a midwife and helped her neighbors bring their babies into the world.

But Grace's mother passed when she was only a teenager. So, Grace had to grow up fast, had to learn fast. It was then up to her and her father to maintain the farm. Her father taught her how to buy and tend livestock, how to plant crops like tobacco and keep them healthy for high yields and good prices. She learned how to dry and store wet grains, to protect them from mold and ruin. Grace's senses were honed to read the weather and the wind.

She did all this while doing the other chores expected of pioneer home makers. From dusk to dawn, she ground corn, milked cows, butchered meat, brewed beer, grew vegetables, made meals, and washed clothes.

So, by the time Grace White married at 20 and became Grace Sherwood, she was wise and responsible beyond her years. As a wedding present, Grace's father gave the young couple 50 acres of land. He passed soon after, leaving them his massive 145-acre farm.

Grace loved working her land. She'd often be seen cultivating the soil to protect her tobacco, wild rice, herbs, and vegetables from the elements or hurricanes.

While she worked, she was often seen wearing trousers — not a dress or a gown expected of women at the time. She was also often seen on the bank of the Asheville River. There, she mixed her healing potions in a bubbling cauldron over an outdoor cook fire.

Grace was also known for the fanciful stories from England and Scotland she'd learned growing up. She'd tell these tales full of magic to local children.

For this and more, Grace Sherwood was called "headstrong," "independent," and "nonconventional."

While Grace worked her farm and told her stories, witches were hanged in the Massachusetts Colony. By 1692, 20 people in Salem had been accused, tried, and executed on charges of witchcraft.

However, the religious fervor of the Puritans was not so widely welcomed around Pungo, Virginia Beach, or even the Commonwealth of Virginia at the time. Religion was to be enjoyed and relied upon but survival was the main goal of many Virginia colonists.

Sorcery and witchcraft — and accusations of both — were as old as time back in the European home countries of these American settlers. For proof, archeologists in 1970s dug up "witch bottles" in Princess Anne County, home of our hardworking, pants-wearing Grace Sherwood. These bottles were folk magic defenses against evil spirits, witches, and magical attack. They were buried beneath the house or displayed in the house in some inconspicuous location.

These little glass bottles would contain iron nails or copper pins meant to captivate an evil spirit and capture it in the bottle. They also contained hair, or fingernails, and the urine of the person in need of protection. Once the spirit was in the bottle, they'd be impaled on the nails and pins and drowned in the urine. Break one of these witch bottles, and the spirit — or the witch — would be released, leaving only havoc and mayhem in its wake.

However, beasties were the first line of defense against evil spirits in colonial Virginia. Horseshoes were hung over the door. Why? Witches hated horses. That's why they rode brooms. That's what the colonials thought. Carvings of squirrels — the day animal — and of owls — the night animal — were left in yards and gardens to protect homes day and night.

Now, the witch trials in Salem concluded in 1692 with no more convictions or executions after the original 20. But it was around this time that rumors began to swirl around Pungo about witchcraft and Grace Sherwood.

The tales were wild. One held that Grace had sailed in an egg shell — you read that right — across the Atlantic to the Mediterranean. There, she'd fallen for the fragrance of rosemary, enough so that she filled her little egg shell boat with it, brought it back to Princess Anne County, and planted it around her place.

That seems like a wild jump, doesn't it? An egg shell boat? Well, when we left Grace, she was working her land and minding her business, wasn't she? Some thought she was minding it too well. Her crops thrived when others failed. Her livestock was healthy when others were sick and dying. It was enough to make some around Pungo jealous, especially women.

Grace learned agriculture from her father, probably the same lessons taught to boys of her age at the time. She was learned and experienced at farming far beyond her years, especially as a woman. So the success of her family's farm might have seemed extraordinary. And there's nothing like success that can make you feel bad if you don't have it and with working with the same basic materials.

Then, there was those pants she wore. Different. Then, there was her healing arts.She knew what herbs would break a fever, maybe, and how to make a just the right poultice to heal a wound. Again, seems like a small and important thing to know now. But these settlers, any settlers or anyone at the time really, didn't understand science, if that was even a word in their vocabulary, then. If they didn't understand it but it worked, it may have seemed like magic to them. And then, just think of Grace sitting on the bank of the Asheville River huddled over her bubbling cauldron.

Then, there were Grace's stories. Those wild tales from the old country with odd and fanciful characters. Now, while the Virginia settlers weren't as Puritanical as those in Massachusetts, these stories did not sit well. And some of the Pungo women decided they did not want their good children to hear Grace's stories.

All of it, together, raised her profile in the community. All of it, together, convinced Grace Sherwood's neighbors that she was in touch with otherworldly and sinister forces. And if she used these for her own success, how long would it be before Grace used her supernatural talents to harm the good folks around Pungo? Once the rumors began, it did not take long for them to become real. Well, real to the judicial system anyways.

Her neighbors had, finally, claimed all of this in public. Grace had bewitched them and they sued her. One woman claimed the Grace had entered her home — her bedroom — had slipped through the keyhole like a cat, tormented her. She said Grace rode the woman her on her back like a horse, and clawed her enough to make blood flow.

The claims were denied. But Grace fought back in 1697 and

1698. Grace and her husband were in court, arguing that those neighbors had slandered her name. They won. But the court forced the Sherwoods to pay for court costs for the nine-day trial. Years passed. Grace's husband passed. But the accusations did not stop.

In 1705, Grace was attacked. A woman found her and badly beat her. She claimed that Grace had bewitched her and her unborn child and caused her to miscarry. Grace proved in court that she home alone that day and her sons were out fishing on the Chesapeake. In court, she showed the scrapes and bruises from the woman and the charges were dropped. Grace was awarded 20 shillings.

Later, neighbors claimed they saw Grace dancing naked, cavorting with the devil by the light of the moon. They said she blighted their cotton crop and killed their livestock. Grace's demon pacts with the devil were evidenced, neighbors said, by her warnings of a coming storm to move their sheep to higher ground. She knew somehow and the thunder and lighting she drew drove them all into a river and drowned. It all was enough evidence for yet another court action.

The county court said the accusations and such a trial to follow them were without precedent. Legal officials at the time urged those against Grace to take their case to the governor's council at Williamsburg.

State officials searched Grace's home. They didn't find a horseshoe above the door, any witch bottles inside the house, nor any amulet anywhere that might've protected Grace or given her any supernatural powers. With this, officials could not approve the burning of the woman at the stake.

But this wasn't enough for those in Princess Anne County. They demanded a trial for Grace Sherwood. But not one in a courtroom. Her purity needed to proved in their God's purest element, water. Grace was ordered to be ducked.

The trial was simple. According to records, they aimed to "put her in water above a man's depth and try her how she swims." If she was a pure as the water, it would take her. If she was innocent, she would drown. If she floated, God's water would reject her, and she was wicked, guilty of witchcraft and all those accusations of her neighbors.

Her original trial date was paused as a storm rolled in. I guess those who ordered her to the water did not want to face the water themselves. So, Grace sat in a timbered jail on a dirt floor with only a straw mattress for comfort.

But they hauled her out on July 10th to be shamed. She was stood upon a pedestal and made to ask forgiveness for being a witch. If she couldn't do that, she was made to ask forgiveness for even accused of being a witch. Authorities hoped she'd confess. To put an end of all of it. But Grace never admitted anything.

She was shackled. Loaded on a cart and carried to a site on Lynnhaven Road, to the picturesque banks of the Lynnhaven River.

"I be not a witch."

Court records said the scene was "still and lonely. Oozy banks skirted with pines and lugubrious cypresses shining in the sun. White-winged sea-fowl flitting and screaming, the far lines of the Chesapeake coast and the dim haze toward the shore of the Atlantic...the waves were lapping in the grass, and the odor of the pines mingled with the scent of rosemary."

Grace was then bound for the trial, her right thumb to her great left toe and her left thumb to her great right toe. And all of it was bound together. The sheriff proclaimed, "I have cross bound the prisoner, Mistress Grace Sherwood." And some from the crowd shouted, "she is guilty! She is a witch! Duck her!"

Grace and the sheriff were lowered into the boat. They made their way into the deepest part of the bay about 200 yards from the bank. Boatmen rowed five other women to the point as well as witnesses and the boats were tied together.

"Mistress Grace, do you have anything to say," the sheriff asked in witness to those gathered in the boats.

"I be not a witch, I be a healer," Grace proclaimed. "Before this day be through, ye will receive a worse ducking than I."

Those five trustworthy women from Pungo checked Grace Sherwood for marks upon her body and any amulets that might protect her in her trial. Finding none, Grace Sherwood was pushed into the dark waters of the Lynnhaven River of the Chesapeake Bay.

Grace sank. Down, down into those murky waters. Onlooker above might've watched the surface of the water, watching the ripples dissipate into a natural stillness. Then, Grace Sherwood emerged from the water, gasping for air and her hair plastered to her forehead. Those ropes were still tied around her body but Grace floated.

Surprised and dismayed, those in the boats around her, tied a 13 pound Bible around Grace's neck. This was meant to help her sink, prove her purity and save her soul. She submerged once again and her neighbors, once again, waited and watched the surface of the water.

Grace emerged again, this time, maybe, with a smile on her face. In her second duck, she'd untied the ropes and set herself free, no matter what that meant, and she was happy. She swam around the bay and laughed at the spectators.

An account at the time said, "For low and behold, Grace Sherwood floated. And the infuriated sorceress promised all who had come to see her trial by water would themselves be saturated." The story goes that the Virginia sky was clear and blue when Grace went into the water. When she was hauled out, the sky turned black, the wind blew in gales, and buckets of rain sent the crowd to their carriages.

The Salem trials had ended 12 years before Grace went into the water that day. Still, she spent seven years in prison after her ducking ordeal. A Virginia governor freed her but with that stain of a witchcraft conviction upon her name.

She didn't care. She wanted her old life back. She called her three boys back from Knott's Island where they'd been staying with relatives. She wanted her farm back, too, and petitioned the government. She paid the fees in tobacco.

With it all, Grace Sherwood made Virginia history twice. She was the first woman to be solely named on deed for land. And she was the last woman — or person — tried for witchcraft in the Commonwealth of Virginia.

After years of peace on her farm with her children, Grace Sherwood passed away in 1740. Her sons buried her on her favorite spot on the Lynhaven River, where she'd made her potions in that bubbling coffin. But the legend around Pungo said Grace simply vanished into thin air. All she left behind was a cloven footprint in the ashes of the fire.

Though so may forgot her name, the Witch of Pungo legend lived on in the area well, right up to present day. In the 70s, a boat named the Witch of Pungo won a race sanctioned by the Chesapeake Bay Yacht Racing Association. Local newspaper headlines referencing Pungo at all tried hard to work the words "witch" into them. A review of Blue Pete's restaurant, for example, was headlined "Pungo place serves bewitching seafood."

A reenactment of Grace's court trials played out in front of tourists at Colonial Williamsburg. When Grace's original house burned in the 90s, it merited a local news story. A Virginia Beach haunted house operator claimed his attraction featured the real-life skull of the Witch of Pungo.

But fast forward a bit and respectable history finally caught up to Grace Sherwood. In 2006, the Witch of Pungo was no longer a witch. On the 300th anniversary of ducking trial — that trial by water — Grace was pardoned by Tim Kaine, then the governor of Virginia.

"With 300 years of hindsight, we all certainly can agree that trial by water is an injustice," Kaine said in a letter at the time. "We also can celebrate the fact that a woman's equality is conditionally protected today and women have the freedom to pursue their hopes and dreams."

Kaine also proclaimed July 10th, to be "Grace Sherwood Day," to "clear the name of a woman whose only sin was she was left a farm, she worked hard, and some of the people didn't like her."

Later, her church, the Old Donation Church in Virginia Beach, dedicated a stone in its herb garden to Grace in 2014. It's the same place Grace was grace was accused of witchcraft 308 years before, where her pastor asked her to admit to witchcraft, but Grace refused.

"Old Donation Church is a little late with this," Bob Perrine, the church's historian said at the time. "But it can never be too late to heal our wounds."

The road to get out to the site where Grace faced that trial is still to this day called Witchduck Point Road. It'll lead you through a fancy neighborhood to a point overlooking the Chesapeake to a spot of water called Witchduck Bay. As far as memorials go, this seems dubious at best.

But Virginia Beach did erect a monument to Grace Sherwood, a real nice memorial this time. Just down the street from the Old Donation Church, a statue of Grace stands. Across the street from a Walgreens, she stares peacefully at the ground, with a bindle of herbs held at her waist.

Milton Keynes UK
Ingram Content Group UK Ltd.
UKHW022341050624
443649UK00018BA/1156